ABOUT TURKEY

Geography, Economy, Politics, Religion, and Culture

Rashid Ergener

Pilgrims' Process, Inc.
Boulder, CO

ABOUT TURKEY:

GEOGRAPHY, ECONOMY, POLITICS, RELIGION, AND CULTURE

ISBN: 0-9710609-6-7

Library of Congress Control Number: 2002108948

Printed in the United States of America

0 9 8 7 6 5 4 3 2 1

Contents

TURKEY, TURKS, ATATURK

Turkey is a young republic situated on a very ancient land. Throughout the ages, several miraculous occurrences took place on the land that is now Turkey. Perhaps the most important of these is the Neolithic revolution, during which our ancestors made the transition from a hunter-gatherer, nomadic existence to sedentary living and food production. The largest known Neolithic settlement is Çatalhöyük, located in central Turkey. This fascinating site possibly had a population of 10,000 as early as the sixth millennium BC.

The land we call Turkey served as a bridge between Asia and Europe. Turks, who originated in Central Asia, arrived in the eleventh century AD and rapidly conquered the land from the Eastern Roman Empire, founding the Seljuk State. Seljuk Turks withstood the Crusades and the Mongol raids but disintegrated shortly thereafter, splitting into sixteen smaller principalities. One of these, the Ottoman, grew to be a world empire.

Spreading over three continents, from the gates of Vienna to the Arab peninsula, the Ottoman Empire covered all of North Africa and all lands around the Black Sea. It was a miraculous accomplishment. But it came to an end as the Ottomans fell behind the advances in science and industry that took place in the West and as the conquered nations rose one by one against their rule. The First World War witnessed the final dissolution of the empire as Arabs mobilized by Lawrence of Arabia rose against the sultan. Turkey, the heartland of the Ottoman Empire, was occupied and partitioned by the allies after the War.

A new miracle—the Turkish Republic—emerged from the ashes of the Ottoman Empire. This miracle would not have been possible if it ere not for the leadership of a single man, Mustafa Kemal Ataturk, a young general at the time and the Turkish hero of the Gallipoli Campaign. He mobilized a war-weary, worn-out nation with a per-capita income of $50 in a campaign against the victors of the First World War, despite the urgings to the contrary of the sultan, the traditional ruler, and his government. Ataturk led his armies brilliantly to victory in a war that was fought against seemingly impossible odds. Following the successful conclusion of the war in 1923 he declared the Turkish Republic and sent the royal family into exile. He then spent the remaining fifteen years of his life as the first president of Turkey, leading the reforms that forged a modern nation out of the debris of a medieval empire.

For the first time in history, Ataturk made a Moslem nation into a secular one. Also for the first time in a Moslem country, he recognized the complete legal equality of women with men. Turkish women could vote and be elected to office before French, Italian, Greek, and Swiss women. He changed the lifestyle of the nation. The weekly holiday was changed from Friday to Sunday. The way people dressed was changed; the red fez was made illegal and the black veil strongly discouraged. Western calendar and measurement systems were adopted.

Even though Ataturk was one of the most brilliant military leaders in history and had the rank of field marshal, (his rank well earned on the field), he never wore a uniform after becoming president and he banned his generals from politics. He also banned all medals, decorations, and aristocratic titles. Unlike his contemporaries Hitler and Mussolini, he never declared himself president for life nor did he interfere in daily government or in the courts, thus laying down the foundations of a democracy. It is part of his legacy that Turkey has been a multi-party democracy since 1946.

Unlike the European dictators who were his contemporaries, Ataturk refused to define nationhood based on race. He introduced the modern concept of nationhood with the statement, "How happy is the one who calls oneself a Turk," meaning that one is a Turk not by race, ethnic group, or religion, but by choice. "A Turk," he said, "is a citizen of the Turkish Republic."

His nation honored him with the name "Ataturk," meaning "father of Turks," when he made it a law that Turks would have second names as well as first, something that they did not have before. He continues to bless his people and to give them affirmation as befits a true father, from his mausoleum in Ankara, where there is not one single word that praises him but, instead, many of his words that praise his beloved people, such as "The right to rule belongs to the people," "Turks are brilliant, Turks are intelligent, Turks are hard working."

This book is an overview of contemporary Turkey, this amazing miracle initiated on a very ancient land by Mustafa Kemal Ataturk.

GEOGRAPHY

Area: Turkey's total area is 814,578 square kilometers, which is slightly larger than Texas. 3% of the country is in Europe, and the rest (790,200 sq. km—97%) in Asia. The section in Asia is called Anatolia, and the section in Europe is called Thrace.

Location: Turkey is approximately 1,600 km (approximately 1000 miles) from east to west and 550 km from north to south. The country is situated between 42 degrees latitude, which passes through Sinop, a port on the Black Sea, and 40 degrees latitude, which passes through the

Beysun village of Hatay province, which is on the Mediterranean, near the Syrian border. The furthest point to the west is the island of Imroz, in the Aegean Sea, 25 degrees longitude. The furthest point to the east is the junction of the Aras and Karasu rivers in the province of Agri, 45 degrees longitude.

Borders: Turkey has borders with Georgia, Armenia, the Nahcevan region of Azerbaijan and Iran in the east, Iraq and Syria to the southeast, and Greece and Bulgaria to the west.

Topography: The European part of Turkey is fertile and hilly. The Asian part consists of an inner high plateau bounded on the north and south by steep mountain ranges that are part of the Alpine-Himalayan system. The plateau starts at sea level at the Aegean shore and rises steadily towards the east, reaching a height of 1700 meters (m)(approximately 5200 feet). The center is a treeless depression at 800–1000 m, containing a large salt lake. Southeast Anatolia is considerably lower and flatter, falling gently from 800 m in the north to about 400 m near the Syrian border. Deep gorges separate the mountain ranges in the south and in the north. The coast is steep along the Mediterranean and the Black Sea.

Seas: The Black Sea lies to the north, the Aegean to the west, and the Mediterranean to the south. Anatolia and Thrace are separated by the straits that are situated in the provinces of Istanbul and Canakkale and by the Sea of Marmara, which lies between the straits. The strait in Istanbul is called the Bosphorus, and the one in Canakkale is called the Dardanelles.

TURKEY'S BORDERS	
Country	Km
Armenia	268
Georgia	252
Azerbaijan (Nahcevan)	9
Bulgaria	240
Greece	206
Iran	499
Iraq	331
Syria	822
TOTAL	2627

TURKEY'S SHORELINE (KM.)				
	Asia	Europe	Islands	Total
Aegean	2593	212	679	3484
Black Sea	1448	177	6	1631
Mediterranean	1542	-	112	1654
Marmara	663	264	252	1179
The Bosphorus	35	55	-	90
The Dardanelles	94	78	-	172
TOTAL	6375	786	1049	8210

Major Rivers: The largest river, the Euphrates (1263 km long), is in the southeast. The Tigris (523 km) is also in the southeast. Both rivers flow into Syria and Iraq. Aras (441 km), which forms part of Turkey's border with Armenia and Coruh (355 km), are the major rivers in the east. The Kizilirmak (1182 km), in central Turkey flows into the Black Sea; it is the longest river to originate in Turkey and reach the sea on the Turkish shore. Yesilirmak (512 km), in central Turkey, and Sakarya (824 km), in the northwest, are the other rivers that flow into the Black Sea. Meric (211 km) originates in Bulgaria and forms Turkey's border with Greece. Gediz (350 km), Kucuk Menderes (140 km), and Buyuk Menderes (529 km) are the major rivers in western Anatolia. Seyhan (560 km) and Ceyhan (509 km) are the major rivers that irrigate the fertile Cukurova plain in the Adana province in southern Turkey.

Climate: All four seasons are experienced in Turkey. Climate is typically Mediterranean with dry summers and rain during the fall and spring. There is more rain along the Mediterranean and Black Sea shores, where mountains are parallel to the shore. In the northeast there is rain throughout the year. In the Aegean region, where mountains are perpendicular to the shore, rain clouds penetrate the country along deep valleys and rainfall is sufficient. Central Turkey and eastern Turkey, which are covered by high mountains, receive relatively less rain. The climate is milder along the shores and the Aegean region. In central Turkey and in the east, the climate is harsher with intense heat during the summer and severe cold and heavy snow during the winter.

YEARLY AVERAGE TEMPERATURES IN VARIOUS REGIONS			
Region	Yearly Average Temperature	Highest Temperature (Centigrade)	Lowest Temperature (Centigrade)
South (Adana)	18.7	44.6	-4.6
Aegean (Izmir)	17.5	42.7	-8.4
Marmara (Istanbul)	13.7	40.6	-13.0
Black Sea (Trabzon)	14.5	38.2	-7.4
Central (Konya)	11.7	40.0	-24.9
East (Van)	8.9	36.7	-28.7
Southeast (Urfa)	18.1	46.5	-12.4

ANNUAL RAINFALL, DAYS WITH SNOW, DAYS WITH FROST (CM)			
Region	Annual Rainfall (cm)	Days with Snow	Days With Frost
South (Antalya)	103.0	0	1.2
Aegean (Izmir)	70.4	0	6.2
Marmara (Istanbul)	78.7	8.2	21.7
Black Sea (Trabzon)	83.1	7.2	8.0
Central (Ankara)	36.0	22.3	85.5
East (Van)	37.8	80.4	132.1
Southeast (Urfa)	46.0	3.1	23.5

POPULATION

POPULATION DENSITY IN SELECTED COUNTRIES			
Country	Population Density	Country	Population Density
Former USSR	13	France	102
Iran	28	Denmark	119
Iraq	38	Italy	191
Bulgaria	81	Belgium	326
Greece	76	Great Britain	235
Spain	77	Germany	250
Turkey	83	Holland	358

Population and Population Density: According to the census held in 2000, Turkey's population is 67 million. The population is expected to reach 88 million by 2025 and to stabilize at 95 million by 2050. Population density is 83 persons per square km.

Population Growth Rate: The average fertility of Turkish women has declined from 8 in 1947, to 3 in 1978, to below 2.5 in 1998, compared with 2.1 in the USA, 1.4 in Japan, 1.3 in Germany, and 1.2 in Italy. It is expected that this rate will drop to 2 by 2010.

Birth rate (births in a given year divided by population) dropped from 6.6% in 1950 to 4.3% in 1965 and to 2% in 2000, compared with 3.2% in poor countries, 1.7% in rich countries, and a world average of 2.9%.

POPULATION GROWTH RATE IN SELECTED COUNTRIES	
Country	Population Growth Rate (%)
Germany	0.1
Holland	0.5
Switzerland	0.59
Ireland	0.7
Portugal	0.9
Turkey	1.47
World Average	1.8

Death rate (deaths in a given year divided by population) also dropped from 1.6% in 1965 to 0.8% in 1989 (world average 1.1%). Since the birth rate has declined faster than the death rate, the population growth rate has also declined, from 2.5% in 1965 to 1.47% in 1997. Population growth rate is expected to fall below 1% by 2015.

Family Size: Average family size is 4.3. 92% of families have children. In Istanbul, 72% of families are nuclear families, composed of parents and children. Family size and fertility of women is higher in rural areas as compared with urban areas and in the western regions as compared with the east. Average family size is 4 in urban and 4.9 in rural areas. Rural families adopt the fertility patterns of urban families within ten years after migrating to urban areas. Rapid urbanization is the main reason behind the drop in the population growth rate. (Sources: State Institute of Statistics; Prof. Emre Kongar, *Life Style and Problems of Istanbul Population,* a study conducted for the Istanbul Chamber of Commerce, 2000.)

Birth Control: Birth control is legal and encouraged by the government. Birth control devices can be obtained freely from government hospitals. There is no outright opposition by the religious establishment to birth control. However, Moslem religion indirectly discourages the use of birth control since the religion encourages the fatalistic attitude "If God gives life, God will take care."

According to a study conducted in 1998 by Hacettepe University Population Studies Institute *(Cumhuriyet Bilim ve Teknik,* October 6, 1999), 97% of families are aware of birth control techniques and 64% practice birth control. Results of this study show that 20% of women use IUDs and 7% of men use condoms. 24% of couples practice timing. According to a study conducted by the Women's Status and Problems Directorate of the Office of the Prime Minister, 40% of those in the cities practice modern birth control techniques and 25.2% practice traditional techniques. The same ratios are 31.4% and 26% respectively in the countryside *(Hürriyet,* September 25, 2001).

Abortion is legal if the doctor regards the pregnancy as a hazard for the mother. According to an opinion poll, 29.3% of Turks approve abortion, 33.7% oppose, and 35.5% oppose for religious reasons (Piar-Gallup Poll, *Radikal,* June 10, 1999). According to the Hacettepe University study, 27% of women have experienced at least one abortion, and 15% of all pregnancies are terminated with abortion (20% in western and 10% in eastern regions). 62% of abortions are realized for birth control purposes.

Age Distribution of Population: Turkey is a very young country. There are 32 million Turks who are younger than 25. Average age is 19.

Age Distribution in Turkey	
Age Group	% in Age Group
15	38.5
15-29	27.7
30-44	16.0
45-59	11.2
60-64	1.8
65+	4.8

66.2% of Turks are younger than 30; half are younger than 22; and 38.5% are younger than 15 (45% in east and southeast Turkey). Only 20% of Europeans are younger than 15. Only

(%) of Population Older than 65 in Selected Countries	
Country or Region	Population Older than 65 (%)
Sweden	18.0
Norway	16.0
Great Britain	15.0
EU	13.0
North America	12.6
Australia	12.1
Turkey	4.8
Asia	4.8
South America	4.6
North Africa	3.8
Central and South Africa	2.7

4.8% of the Turkish population is older than 65.

Life Expectancy: Average life expectancy is 72 (74 for females and 69 for males). The population is very young. There are 32 million Turks who are younger than 25.

Life Expectancy in Selected Countries	
Country	Average Life Expectancy
France	79
Japan	78
Greece	78
Australia	77
Canada	77
Hong Kong	77
Italy	77
Spain	77
Sweden	77
UK	77
Israel	76
USA	76
Germany	75
Turkey	72
Zambia	53
Bangladesh	50

Physical Features of Turks: 48.6% of Turks have light brown complexion, 25.8% have dark, and 25.6% have fair complexion. The dominant complexion is auburn. 64% have straight hair. The average height of a male is 1.72 m and the average height of a female is 1.62 m The average weight of a man is 71.6 kg and the average weight of women is 61.2 kg 35.5% of Turks have A RH+ blood type. Average shoe size is 42 for men and 37 for women. 62% of males have moustaches and 19% have beards. (Piar-Gallup Poll, *Hürriyet*, June 10, 1999.) 58% in the Aegean, Marmara, and Mediterranean regions have blue or green eye color, whereas 63% in the central, eastern, and southeastern regions have dark eye color. 48% have thick eyebrows. In the Aegean, eastern Marmara, and Mediterranean regions, the nose is straight, similar to the Hellenistic nose; and the nose is arched on the Black Sea. (Prof. Erdogan Cireli, Aegean University Faculty of Medicine, Morphology Department.)

CITIES

Urbanization: Presently, 74% of the population lives in urban areas. Urbanization is proceeding very rapidly. The percentage of the population living in urban areas was 44% in 1980, 32% in 1960, 25% in 1950, and 20% in 1923. During the years 1980–90, the urban population increased at the rate of 4.5% annually whereas rural population increased at the rate of 1%. In 1997, the same ratios were 3% and –6.5% respectively. By the year 2015, 84.5% of the population will be living in urban areas. According to the census held in 2000, the largest cities are Istanbul (10 million), Ankara (3.5 million) and Izmir (3 million). (Sources: State Institute of Statistics, *UN Human Development Indices 2000.*)

Gecekondus: Because of continuous rural-urban migration (320 persons immigrate daily to Istanbul and 220 to Izmir), all major cities are surrounded by shantytowns inhabited by immigrants. Shantytown houses are called *gecekondus*. This word literally means "built over-night." The shell of a shantytown house is built "overnight" by its owner, with the help of friends and relatives. According to an ancient Ottoman custom, houses built overnight couldn't be torn down. (Jews under the colonial administration in Palestine took advantage of the same law in starting new settlements.) Construction of *gecekondus* continues, despite the clear legal ban introduced in 1966.

65% of all buildings in Turkey are *gecekondus* and 35% of the urban population lives in *gecekondus*. 94% of *gecekondus* are built on government land: 51% are on land belonging to central government and 43% on municipal land. 55% of all land in Turkey is government owned (as compared to 15% on the average in Western countries), inherited by the governments of the Turkish Republic from the Ottoman Crown. In most cases, the allocation of government land among newcomers is determined by the so-called "real-estate Mafia." 78% of current *gecekondu* builders obtain land from the "Mafia." The profits derived by the "Mafia" from the allocation of government land are estimated to be around a half billion dollars annually. From the economic point of view, the *gecekondu* is an expensive form of settling newcomers in urban areas. Many *gecekondus* are built on hilly terrain and without prior planning. Construction of municipal services for *gecekondu* areas is therefore very costly.

The high economic costs of *gecekondus* are perhaps made up for by the social benefits of this form of settlement. Above all, a gecekondu eliminates the "homeless" problem and anchors the uprooted migrant within the system. A *gecekondu* owner has hope: his one-floor residence will eventually turn into an apartment from which he can collect rent. According to a study conducted for the State Planning Organization (Istiklal Alpar, Samira Yener, 1992), 45% of *gecekondus* have two or more floors. A *gecekondu* also helps to reduce the psychological tensions created by migration to an urban center. A typical *gecekondu* is a village-type one-floor house with a small garden. It is easier for newcomers to urban areas to adapt themselves to their new lifestyle when living in such housing, as compared with living in apartment blocks. Furthermore, immigrants from a particular village or town tend to settle together in the same *gecekondu* neighborhood. Close social ties and controls, which continue to operate in this setting, help to reduce alienation and contribute to lower crime rate.

Standard of Living in *Gecekondus*: The standard of living in *gecekondus* is not as low as one might expect. 30% of all household goods sold in Turkey are purchased by Istanbul *gecekondus* dwellers (Biltin Toker, Kent Dinamikleri Enstitusu.) 18% of *gecekondu* residents own cars. 56% of *gecekondu* residents are workers and 7% are unemployed. (*Milliyet* August 16, 1999.)

Istanbul Population: Istanbul has always been a large city. The population of Istanbul was half a million during the sixth century AD, under Byzantine Emperor Justinian. During the seventeenth century, in order to reduce the inflated population of the city, the Ottoman Sultan Murat IV took the drastic measure of forcefully moving 150,000 residents who had migrated to the city without prior permission, to the Balkans.

The current population of Istanbul is 10 million. This means that one out of every seven Turks lives in Istanbul. Whereas the population density is 81 persons per sq. km for Turkey as a whole, population density in Istanbul is 1,700 persons per sq. km. Istanbul's population grows at the rate of 3.5% annually. This rate is more than twice as high as the rate of growth of Turkey's population as a whole (1.47%). The high rate of population growth in Istanbul is largely due to migration from the countryside. Only 29% of Istanbul residents are born in this city. The remaining 71% are migrants. Only 17% of Istanbul residents have ancestors who have been living in the city since before 1945. 13% of Istanbul residents were born in east or southeast Turkey. Since most migrants are single, there are 2,800,000 singles (above age 12) living in Istanbul. 400,000 of those are women. The high rate of population growth necessitates continuous new housing construction. Profits generated by land speculation in Istanbul are estimated to be equal to Turkey's national budget.

The city has 54 municipalities and extends 100 km from east to west and 30 km from north to south. There are 160,000 businesses, 7,400 factories, 1,300 bank branch offices, 4,224 pubs, 1,000 hotels, 70 cinemas, 12 universities, 2,647 schools, and 100 hospitals in the city. 303 newspapers and 495 periodicals are published in Istanbul. 1,500,000 motor vehicles are registered, and 300 more join the traffic daily. Each day, the city produces 7,000 tons of solid and 1 million cubic meters of liquid wastes.

Istanbul *Gecekondus*: 65% of Istanbul's population lives in *gecekondus*. The number of *gecekondus* in Istanbul (approximately one million) is two times higher than the number of legal residences. Daily, 220 *gecekondus* are built in Istanbul. This figure is five times higher than the number of legal residences constructed daily in Istanbul. 56% of *gecekondus* are built on government land. 30% of all household goods sold in Turkey are purchased by Istanbul *gecekondus* dwellers. (Biltin Toker, *Kent Dinamikleri Enstitusu.)*

Istanbul Economy: 27.5% of Turkey's national product is produced in Istanbul, and 40% of all tax collected in Turkey is collected in Istanbul. 38% of Turkey's industrial firms and 55% of Turkey's commercial firms are concentrated in Istanbul. The income annually produced in Istanbul is equal to 1.5 times the GNP of Romania, 2.5 times the GNP of Syria, 4.5 times the GNP of Bulgaria, and 21.5 times the GNP of Armenia. A total of 1,500,000 workers employed in 7400 factories produce a quarter of Turkey's manufacturing output. 55% of Turkish textile production, 55% of Turkish chemical goods production, and 50% of Turkey's metal goods production take place in Istanbul. One-fifth of Turkey's exports and one-third of Turkey's imports are handled through Istanbul's 40,000 export and 30,000 import companies.

SOCIAL SECURITY AND HEALTH

Social Security: Government bureaucrats, employees working under contract, and the self-employed are covered under separate, centralized, and compulsory social insurance programs (both pension and health). Under these arrangements, insurance coverage continues as one changes jobs. Government-organized insurance programs do not cover 6 million workers employed mainly on family farms (60% of all workers, 75% of all female workers).

Turkey allocates 12% of the national budget to social security. Other countries allocate up to 53%. The government provides 2.8% of the social-security budget. This ratio is 19.75% in Canada, 23.68% in Germany, 25.8% in Austria, 28.73% in France and 35.39% in Finland (*Cumhuriyet*, July 13, 1999.) 33.5% of workers' salaries are withheld as social security payments. This is the highest rate in the world compared with 21% in Germany, 12% in Spain, and 10% in Japan). Employers' dues to the system have been cancelled on many occasions. Social security suffers heavy losses due to poor management of funds and the delays in the payments of dues by employers.

SHARE OF SOCIAL SECURITY IN THE BUDGET	
Country	Share of Social Security in Government Budget
Sweden	53%
Germany	46%
World Average	35%
UK	33%
USA	32%
Turkey	12%

Retirement: The social-security system has been the subject of a major controversy during recent years. Under the previous system, which was in effect until 1999, male civil servants could retire after 25 years provided that they were older than 55; female civil servants could retire after 20 years, provided that they were older than 50. Employees working under contract could retire after 5,000 workdays with 20 years of minimum employment for women and 25 years of minimum employment for men. Under this system, it was possible for women working under contract to retire at the age of 38 and for men working under contract to retire at the age of 43. On the average, it was possible for someone who had worked for 25 years to receive retirement and health benefits for 16 years.

RETIREMENT AGE IN SELECTED COUNTRIES					
Country	Female	Male	Country	Female	Male
Denmark	67	67	Chile	60	65
Germany	65	65	EU Average	60.4	64.2
Japan	65	65	France	60	60
USA	65	65	Italy	55	60
Spain	65	65	Jordan	55	60
Portugal	62	65	Kenya	55	60
Belgium	60	65	Pakistan	55	60
Holland	60	65	Sudan	55	60
UK	60	65	Syria	55	60
Greece	60	65	Turkey*	38	43

* Until 1999

A new law enacted in 1999 raised retirement age to 58 for women and 60 for men. Compulsory retirement age from government work was kept at 65.

Supporters of the change point out that retirement age was lower in Turkey than other countries. Their opponents point out that life expectancy is also lower in Turkey and that the raising of retirement requirements practically means retirement in the grave. However, Turks who live beyond the age of 50 have an average life expectancy of 25 more years. Critics of the new system maintain that under former arrangements, only 1% of those who retired were younger than 39, that the median age of retired population was 57, and that the median age of those who retired in 1996 was 50. Only 7% of all retirees are younger than 45 and 1% are younger than 40. Average age of retirement is 50 (51 for men, 47 for women) and average age of retirees is 57. Retired men will have completed 80% of their lives, compared with 83% in Greece, 84% in Germany, 86% in the UK, and 79% in the Philippines. Retired women will have completed 67% of their lives, compared with 87% in Greece, 84% in Germany, 79% in the UK, and 78% in the Philippines. (Ayse Peker, Turkish Central Bank Research Department, 1997.)

Supporters of the present system point out that under previous arrangements two active workers supported one pensioner and that in order to achieve actuarial balance, this ratio should be raised to six to one. (The limit accepted by international labor organizations is four to one.) Supporters of the previous system point out that the ratio is not much different in other countries. Supporters of the change in Turkey's social security system claim that the system was bankrupt and that raising the retirement age was inevitable. Critics of change point out that Turkey should not limit but increase its social-security spending. Turkey spends only 5% of its GNP on social security whereas Sweden spends 38%, Germany 25%, Bulgaria 20%, and the USA 10.5%.

RATIO OF ACTIVE WORKERS TO PENSIONERS			
Country	Active Worker/ Pensioner Ratio	Country	Active Worker/ Pensioner Ratio
Turkey	1,81	Holland	2.50
Italy	1.94	France	2.60
Greece	2,03	England	2.91
Germany	2.13	Finland	3.10
Spain	2.21	Portugal	3.15

Health System: The Turkish health system is rated highly by the World Bank and the United Nations. 91% of the population has access to the health system and 91% to medicine. Preventive medicine reaches 94% of the population; this ratio is 85% in the countryside. 76% of the children in the west and 41% in the east are vaccinated.

Government hospitals provide free health care for all civil servants. Also, the very poor can get free health care in government hospitals. Government-organized, centralized insurance plans covering employees working under contract and the self-employed also provide free health care for their members. Health care can also be purchased through private hospitals and clinics, and it is possible to purchase private health insurance.

There are more than 1000 hospitals. About 720 are operated by the government and 120 by the government-controlled workers' insurance plan. More than 200 hospitals are privately owned. The government encourages private investment in health through tax breaks and subsidies.

There is one hospital bed for every 396 persons. The same ratio is about four times higher in Western European countries. The doctor/population ratio is 1 to 852. The number of persons per dentist is 3,900.

Health expenditures per-capita according to purchasing power parity were $259 in1997. (The EU average is $1,698; $4,095 in the USA, $2,364 in Germany, $2,175 in Canada, $2,047 in France, $1,909 in Australia, $1,760 in Japan, $1,613 in Italy, $1,391 in the UK, $1,246 in Ireland, $1,196 in Greece, and $363 in Mexico.)

During 1960–1997, per-capita expenditures on health rose 11 times. During the same period, per-capita

DOCTOR/POPULATION RATIO IN SELECTED COUNTRIES	
Country	Doctor/Population Ratio
Greece	303
Spain	315
Portugal	345
Denmark	370
Germany	370
Turkey	852

expenditures on health increased 85 times in Spain, 68 times in Japan, 56 times in Greece, 33 times in Belgium and Italy, 32 times in Ireland, 28.5 times in France, 27.5 times in the USA, 26 times in Germany, 20 times in Australia and Canada, and 15 times in New Zealand.

In 1995, 4.2% of the GNP was spent on health compared with 14% in the USA, 10.5% in Germany, 9.7% in France, 9.2% in Canada, 8.6% in Australia, 7.6% in Italy, 7.2% in New Zealand, 6.9% in the UK, 6.5% in Ireland, and 6% in Greece. Expenditures on health are 2.7% of the national budget (7% in Greece, 9% in Portugal, 15% in Holland, 16% in France, and 17% in Germany). The government pays 65% of total expenditures on health compared with 84% in the UK, 83% in Greece, 81% in Ireland and France, 78% in Japan and Germany, 76% in New Zealand, 71% in Canada, 67% in Australia, and 44% in the USA.) (Source: Compiled by Dr. Ali Rizaser, *Cumhuriyet Bilim ve Teknik*, August 18, 2001.)

Causes of Death: Among adults, 38% of deaths are due to coronary problems, 11.5% to cancer, 11.5% to traffic accidents, 3.8% to respiratory infections, and 3.5% to infectious diseases.

Infant Mortality: 3.8% of babies die before reaching age 1. The same ratio is 1.1% for the EU and 3% for countries in the same income group as Turkey. The good news is that infant mortality is declining very rapidly. The present infant mortality rate is less than a quarter of what it was 20 years ago.

10% of infant deaths are due to diarrhea and about 20% is due to infections of the respiratory system. The most important determinant of infant mortality is the mother's education level. Chances of survival of the baby of a college graduate are 5 times higher than the chances of survival for the baby of an illiterate mother. The rate of death among mothers when giving birth is 2.8%. 37% of mothers receive no medical assistance during pregnancy. 19% of births (70% in the east) take place without proper medical assistance. Infant mortality in the countryside is 1.5 times higher than infant mortality in cities, and infant mortality in the east is 1.6 times higher than in the west.

WOMEN

Civic Rights: Under the law there is complete equality of men and women. Turkish civil law, which was adopted from the Swiss civil law in 1926, allows a man to have only one wife and gives women equal rights with respect to inheritance and in other spheres of social life. This is in sharp contrast with the Moslem code, which allows a husband to have four wives, recognizes the testimony of two women as being equal to that of a single man, and gives daughters only half as much inheritance as sons.

Even though the status of women in Turkish society has greatly improved as compared with the past, ancient traditions survive. 59% of Turkish women and 32% of Turkish men believe that it is more difficult to live as a woman than a man in Turkish society. 85% of Turkish women and 75% of Turkish men believe that women in Turkey are repressed. 58% of Turkish men and 62% of Turkish women believe that the legal system discriminates against women. (*Tempo*, January 5–11, 1992.)

Women in Politics: Turkish women received the right to vote and the right to be elected to office at the relatively early date of 1934, before Swiss, Greek, French, and Italian women. Currently, Turkey has several female members of parliament, mayors, and governors. Tansu Ciller, a 46-year-old professor of economics, became Turkey's first female prime minister in 1993. In 1997, there were four female members in the Turkish cabinet, holding the portfolios of family affairs ministry, foreign ministry, interior ministry, and treasury ministry.

During World War II, there were 12 female members of the Turkish parliament, which was more than the number of women in the US Congress at the time. 4% of the parliament members elected in 1999 were women. The same ratio is 3% for Middle Eastern countries, 8% for African countries, and 18% for industrialized nations. 40% of the Swedish, Danish, and Norwegian parliaments, and 30% of New Zealand, South African, and German parliaments, are women. 1.4% of city council members and 5.5% of mayors are women. *(Women in Turkey in 2001,* by the Office of the Prime Minister.)

SUFFRAGE FOR WOMEN			
Country	Year	Country	Year
New Zealand	1893	Spain	1931
Australia	1901	Turkey	1934
Denmark	1915	France	1944
Soviet Union	1917	Italy	1945
Austria	1918	Japan	1945
Canada	1918	Belgium	1948
Germany	1918	Greece	1951
UK	1918	Mexico	1953
Poland	1918	Egypt	1956
Holland	1919	Morocco	1963
Norway	1919	Iran	1963
Sri Lanka	1931	Switzerland	1971

WOMEN'S PARTICIPATION IN LABOR FORCE	
Level of Education	Percentage Working (%)
Illiterate	1.5
Elementary	5
Junior High	12.5
High School	30
Vocational High School	52
College or University	70

Women in the Labor Force: 37% of the labor force is female. This ratio is 48% in Sweden, 46% in the USA, 44% in New Zealand, 43% in Australia, 41% in Japan, 41% in Germany, 38% in Italy, 37% in Greece, 34% in Israel, and 29% in Egypt. 54% of working women are not covered by an insurance program.

Types of Employment: 34% of government-employed doctors, 20% of judges and prosecutors, 21.6% of lawyers, 21% of public notaries, 35% of all bank employees, 33% of civil servants, and half of all teachers are women. The first-ever female Supreme Court justice was Melahat Ruacan, who was appointed in 1954. The first-ever female combat pilot in the world was also Turkish: Sabiha Gokcen joined the service in 1934. 16 out of 225 ambassadors serving in the Turkish Foreign Ministry, including the Turkish ambassador to the Vatican, are women. *(Women in Turkey in 2001,* by the Office of the Prime Minister.)

36% of university faculty is female as compared with 35% in the USA and 18% in Germany. 25% of professors are women, as compared with 13% in the former Yugoslavia, 8% in the former USSR, 5% in Greece, and 3% in Germany. 31% of associate professors, 27% of assistant professors, 30% of lecturers, 54% of instructors, and 34% of research assistants are women. In 2000, presidents of three universities (Istanbul Technical, Marmara, and Bilgi, all located in Istanbul) out of 79 and deans of 49 out of approximately 500 faculties were female.

14% of the members of the Turkish Academy of Sciences are women. 14.6% of those in senior scientific positions are women, as compared to: Iceland 12.3%, New Zealand 7.3%, Ireland 6.4%, US 6.2%, Canada 5.3%, China 5.1%, Scotland 4.5%, Germany 4%, France 3.6%, UK 3.6%, Spain 2.7%, Italy 2.6%, Russia 1.7%, Japan 0.8, and The Netherlands 0.4%. (Source: Natasha Loder, "Gender Discrimination 'Undermines Science" *Nature*, Nov 25, 1999, 402:337.) 10.7% of those employed in internet-related jobs are women, as compared with 14% in Greece, 9.1% in France, 6.5% in the UK, 5.3% in Germany, and 4.5% in Russia (Source: Cisco Systems for International Data Corporation).

9% of working women are either in managerial positions or are self-employed. This ratio is 42% for the USA and 14.1% for the world as a whole. It is expected that the number of businesses owned by females will rise by 100% during the course of next decade (Hasan Gemici, Minister of Family Affairs; *Sabah*, June 20, 1999; *Tempo* December 9-15, 1999). 6.6% of mangers in business (*Tempo*, 626, 1999) and 29% of those in civil service are women.

56.8% of working women are employed in farms, which are mostly family owned. 78% of those who work on the fields are women. 14.4% of working women are employed in industry and 28.9% in the services, compared with 77% in the USA. 10% of urban women (17% in Istanbul and Ankara) who are older than 18 have paid jobs. *(UN Human Development Indices 2001.)*

5.5 million women work on farms as opposed to 1.5 million men. 90% of the workers in hazelnut fields in the Black Sea region and 80% of the workers in cotton fields in the Mediterranean region are women.

13.6% of all industrial workers and 10% of all those employed in service industries are women. 34.7% of the workers in the textiles industry and 60% of the workers in the food processing industry are women. It is expected that employment of women in industrial work will rise by 29.9% during the course of next decade whereas the employment of men will rise by 26.8%. During the same period, employment of women in service industries will rise by 55% and of men by 22%. (*Sabah*, June 20, 1999.)

Wage Discrimination: Even though employers are forbidden by law to discriminate with regard to sex, race, age, and religion, in practice, wages received by women are on the average 30% lower than the wages received by men. This is partly because women are expected to leave the labor force after marriage.

Marriage and Women's Participation in the Labor Force: Employers may be justified in their expectation that married women are likely to leave the labor force due to family obligations. 71% of working women are in the 12–34 age group, while most women older than 30 leave the labor force.

According to a survey conducted for TUSIAD (Association of Turkish Businessmen and Industrialists), 76% of Turkish men do not want their wives to have jobs and 59% do not allow them to work. In 46.4% of families, only one member works. In 19.4% of families, two members work.

88% of the Turkish people believe that "woman means home and children." According to the same study, 52% of Turkish people believe that it is more important for a husband to have a job than the wife. Interestingly, according to the same study, 86% of Turkish people believe that the wife should contribute to the household income as well as the husband, and 45% of Turkish people believe that a woman should have a job in order to gain her independence.

Urbanization, Education, and Women's Participation in the Labor Force: Urbanization, income, and educational are the most important determinants of women's participation in the labor force. 43% of working women live in the three largest cities: Istanbul, Ankara, and Izmir. 15% of women in the top income bracket of urban families are "housewives" as compared with 31% of those who are in the lowest income bracket (VERI ARASTIRMA A.S., *Kentsel Turkiye Raporu, Report on Urban Turkey*). Whereas only 15% of male workers have high school and 8% have college degrees, 30% of female workers have completed high school, and 14% have college degrees. Note that 5% of women and 9% of men have college degrees. An increase in Turkish women's participation in the more advanced spheres of working life should be expected in the near future. The number of female college graduates is rising by 13.3% annually, whereas the number of male college graduates is rising by 8.2%. Currently, 42% of all college students are women, up from 26% in 1980. In 2001, 41% of those who applied to college and 43% of those admitted were females. At many colleges, half the students in fields such as physics and chemistry are females. After the extension of compulsory education to eight years, the number of female students continuing with their education after the sixth grade rose by 69% in

2000, as compared with 1997. This increase should lead to a further rise in the enrollment of female students at the college level.

THE TURKISH FAMILY

Marriage Age: According to the new civic code accepted by the Turkish Parliament in 2001, minimum marriage age, which was previously seventeen for men and fifteen for girls, was raised to eighteen. The average age at marriage is 24 for men and 19.5 for women. It is 27 and 25 respectively in the USA. Average age at marriage is rising. Turkish women in the 45–49 ages were married at the average age of 18.4. The average marriage age is 20.4 for women in the 25–29 age group. The average marriage age for men in the same age group is 24. (ADTAD Report, *Cumhuriyet*, April 25, 2001.) 30% of women older than 30 are married and have children. Marriage age is positively correlated with level of education. The average marriage age of women from the east is 2 years lower than those in the west and average marriage age of men from the east is 1 year lower than those from the west. (Hacettepe University Study, *Cumhuriyet Bilim ve Teknik*, October 6, 1999.)

AVERAGE MARRIAGE AGE FOR FEMALES	
Country	Age
Sweden	28.0
Denmark	27.0
Switzerland	26.0
Tunisia	21.1
Turkey	20.0
Jordan	19.6
Egypt	19.2

Arranged Marriages: 58% of weddings are arranged (Women's Status and Problems Directorate of the Office of the Prime Minister, *Hürriyet*, September 25, 2001.) Arranged marriages are more widespread in rural areas than in cities. In most cases, "arranged" simply means "introduced by the family," the marriage taking place with the approval by the couple.

Marriage Contract: Civic codes of Islam or of other religions are not valid in Turkey, which is a secular country. Therefore, weddings conducted according to a Moslem or other religious code are not legally binding. Only the civil wedding, conducted by the municipal authority or by the census officer, has legal validity. Despite that, 15% of married couples are bound by the religious ceremony only. 81% have both the civic and the religious ceremony. Only 4% have only the civic ceremony. 0.22% live together without a wedding contract. (Family Research Institute of the Office of Prime Minister, *Takvim*, May 30, 2000.) According to a study by the Women's Status and Problems Directorate of the Office of the Prime Minister, 3.8% of couples have only the civic wedding, 7.4% have only the religious wedding, and 88.5% have both. (*Hürriyet*, September 25, 2001) According to the Turkish civil code, a man can have only one wife, yet according to a survey conducted in 1992, 1.1% of the males in cities and 2.2% of males in rural areas have more than one wife (*Milliyet* March 9, 1992).

According to the revisions in the civic code accepted by the Turkish Parliament in 2001, husband and wife have equal say in family affairs. The spouses should jointly decide on the choice of family home, on financial matters, and about the future of children. Spouses jointly contribute to family expenses on the basis of their property and income. Wives are able to use their own family name together with their husband's family name. Chidren born out of wedlock have equal share in inheritance. Spouses are free to seek employment. Marriage with adopted childen is not allowed.

Divorce and Alimony: 95% of those who enter into a wedding contract are marrying for the first time. The marriage rate is 76% and the divorce rate is 15%. (The marriage rate is estimated as the percentage of those above 15 who get married annually and the divorce rate is estimated as the percentage of those who get divorced annually.) The divorce rate is 40% in Europe. 7% of married couples eventually get divorced. 76% of divorces take place in urban centers. The total number of divorces increases by 4–5% annually. The increase between 1986 to 1998 was 187%.

Divorce is obtained through the court. Divorce is easily granted if both sides are willing but is more difficult if one partner (particularly the wife) is reluctant. The custody of young children is usually given to the mother. There has always been alimony. Division of property following divorce was introduced by the new civic code accepted by the parliament in 2002. According to this law, following a divorce, division of property will take place according to the agreement made by the couple prior to the signing of the marriage contract. During the years that preceded the promulgation of this law, courts had effectively introduced division of property by granting high alimony and compensation claims.

Divorces are far more frequent in the western regions of the country than in the east. Half the divorces take place during the first five years of marriage. 45% of the couples that divorce do not have children. 60% of males who seek divorce are 25–39 years old and 60% of females who seek divorce are 20–34 years old. (Cengiz Hortoglu, quoted by Elif Korac, *Milliyet* August 31, 2001.)

Officially, 93.8% of divorces are caused by marital disagreement, 2.2% by desertion, and 0.6% by adultery. "Marital disagreement" is usually a term that disguises other underlying causes for divorce. The findings of the survey conducted by the Office of the Prime Minister in 1996 on 427 subjects on the "true" causes for divorce are given in the following table. The divorce rate declines as the number of children in the family increases. 26% of the women covered under the above study declined to divorce because they had children.

CAUSES FOR DIVORCE	
Cause	%
"Bad Habits"	23
"Exploiting the Spouse"	19
Adultery	16
"Lack of Cultural and Social Cohesion"	11
"Lack of Sexual Cohesion"	7

Domestic Violence: According to the Turkish Family Foundation, 20% of Turkish women are subjected to domestic violence and only 2% of those subjected to violence complain to the police. Note that 16% of American women and 20% of German women encounter violent behavior from their partners. (*Cumhuriyet*, December 18, 1994.) According to a survey (*Hürriyet*, November 18, 1990), 48.5% of Turkish households know of at least one husband who beats his wife. In a study conducted by the Family Research Institute of the Office of the Prime Minister, 27% of those surveyed believe that a husband has the right to beat his wife, 64% think that he does not, and 8.9% do not have an opinion.

Housework: Turkish husbands share very little of the housework, and the children are brought up mainly by their mothers. It is estimated that a working woman, on the average, spends 3.6 hours working at home each day in addition to the 8.8 hours she spends at work.

Adultery: According to a study conducted for *Tempo* magazine, 70% of Turkish men and 72% of Turkish women do not approve of adultery (*Tempo*, January 5–11, 1992). Yet, according to the same survey, 43% of those surveyed know of at least one woman and 62% know of at least one man who they think has committed adultery. The same study indicates that 28% of men and 21% of women have considered committing adultery at some time in their lives.

Premarital Sex: Chastity is still important for a large segment of the population. According to the study referred to above, chastity is important for 53% of Turkish women and 39% of Turkish men (*Tempo*, January 5–11, 1992). According to the same study, 73% of men and 54% of women do not approve of unmarried women having sex.

Very few babies are born out of wedlock. By comparison, almost half the children in Europe are born to couples that are not married. This ratio is 66% in Iceland and 50% in Norway and Denmark.

Because of the limitations on sex before marriage, 48% of young men and 12% of young women masturbate. About 60% of young people learn about sex through their friends. 55% of all women have their first sexual experience with their husbands. 20% of all women report that they are not comfortable with sexual relations. (*Tempo*, January 5-11, 1992.)

33% of young men have their first sexual experience at bordellos (*Tempo*, January 5-11, 1992). There are government-inspected bordellos in most Turkish cities. Women working in these houses are required to have a weekly medical inspection.

EDUCATION

School System: Children start elementary school at the age of six. Preliminary education is eight years. Above the preliminary level, there are three years of high school and four years of college. A master's degree usually requires two years to complete and a doctorate degree takes four years after graduating from college.

The school year ends in June and starts again in September. There is a two-week semester break in February. The school system is mixed gender, though there are a few traditional high schools that are exclusively for male or female students.

The average number of students per instructor is 31 in elementary school, 22 in secondary education, and 21 in post-secondary education. The number of instructors increased by 6.7% annually during 1960–1980 and by 2.9% during 1980–1989.

The government provides free preliminary and secondary education. College students pay a small portion of their costs. Private education is also available. 8% of children are in private preliminary and secondary schools.

Literacy Rate: According to a study conducted by A&G Research Company, 88% of the population is literate (*Hürriyet*, June 10, 1999). 95% of all males and 81% of all females are literate. Literacy rate is positively correlated with income and negatively correlated with age: Whereas 80% of men and 50% of women in the 50–54 age group are literate, 99% of males and 96% of females in the 15–20 age

LITERACY RATES IN SELECTED COUNTRIES	
Country	Literacy Rate (%)
UK	99
USA	99
Spain	98
Cuba	96
South Korea	96
Argentina	94
Chile	91
Turkey	88
Venezuela	85
Mexico	83
Pakistan	35
Afghanistan	29

group are literate. Literacy is higher in urban areas than in rural areas and in western regions as compared with eastern regions.

Years of Schooling: Until recently, Turkey was one of 12 countries in the world where education was compulsory only up to the elementary school level. Consequently, as of 1994, the average years of schooling of Turkish citizens was 4.5. Compulsory education was extended to eight years in 1997, and the average years of schooling of Turkish citizens has been rising ever since. In 2001, the rate of schooling was 94% at the high school level. This ratio was 54.7% before the extension of compulsory education to eight years (Sedat Ergin, *Hürriyet*, Oct 30, 2001).

AVERAGE YEARS OF SCHOOLING N SELECTED COUNTRIES			
Country	Years of Schooling	Country	Years of Schooling
USA	12.3	Greece	6.9
Canada	12.1	Malaysia	5.3
France	11.6	Turkey	4.5
UK	11.5	Brazil	3.9
Australia	11.5	South Africa	3.9
Germany	11.1	Thailand	3.8
Japan	10.7	India	2.4
New Zealand	10.4	Pakistan	1.9

LEVEL OF EDUCATION IN SELECTED ORGANIZATION FOR ECONOMIC COOPERATION AND DEVELOPMENT (OECD) COUNTRIES			
Country	(%) of Population only with Elementary Education	(%) of Population with Secondary School Education	(%) of Population with Post-Secondary Degrees
USA	7	47	36
Germany	18	60	22
Canada	24	36	40
UK	35	49	16
France	49	35	15
Turkey	43	33	7

Child Labor: Despite the legal requirement, in 1996, 13% of Turkish children who were of elementary school age were not attending school (*Cumhuriyet*, February 5, 1996.) This ratio was 29.7% for working class families (*Milliyet* September 1, 1996). In 1989 10.6% of children who attended school also participated in the labor force (*Milliyet* September 1, 1989).

According to the International Labor Organization (ILO), in 1995 more than 1 million Turkish children were working as apprentices. According to the 1999 World Development Indicators, 22% of all children in the 10–14 age group work. According to State Institute of Statistics, children in the 10–14 age group constitute 5% of Turkey's labor force. 32% of children are employed at home industries and 80% in the "non-official" sector, the activities of which are not recorded. 77% of children work in agriculture, 11% in industry, 7% in services, and 5% in trade.

Post-Secondary Education: There are 79 universities, compared with approximately 3500 in the USA and 500 in Japan. Istanbul University is the largest. 19 universities (26%) are owned by private, non-profit organizations; by comparison, 54% of universities and colleges in the USA and 72% of those in Japan are private. Only 5% of students starting college were admitted to private institutions in 2001.

SCHOOLING IN POST-SECONDARY EDUCATION			
Country	(%)	Country	(%)
USA	84	Greece	29
Canada	70	Turkey	28
South Korea	46	Russia	24
France	40	UK	23
Japan	39	Egypt	20
Singapore	38	Syria	18
Germany	33	Mexico	14
Italy	31	Brazil	12

University admissions are based on a central examination. Only 40% of those who apply are graduates of the current year. In 2001, 32% of those who took the exam were admitted to degree programs. 36% of those admitted were admitted to four-year programs, 26% to two-year programs, and 38% to distant education programs.

POST-SECONDARY STUDENTS IN DISTANT EDUCATION	
Country	(%) of Post-secondary Students in Distant Education
Japan	1.6
Germany	3
Spain	12
UK	17
Israel	19
South Korea	30
Turkey	38
Thailand	45

The rate of schooling in post-secondary education is 28%. 35% of post-secondary students are in external or distance-education programs that do not require attendance. Excluding those in external or distance-education programs, the rate of schooling in higher education is 17.9%, which is close to the world average of 19.5%. 8% of all Turkish students receive post-secondary education, while 20% do in EU countries. 5% of women and 9% of men have college degrees.

Approximately 40,000 Turkish students continue post-secondary education programs abroad. About fifteen to twenty thousand are in the US. The annual contribution of Turkish students to the US economy is estimated to be $836 million spent on tuition, fees, and living expenditures, $209 million in taxes, and 10,678 jobs (David Louscher and Alethia Cook, Contribution of Turkish Students to the US Economy, *Foresight International, Milliyet* April 2, 2001). Since 1996, 3,000 students have enrolled in doctorate programs abroad. Half of these have not come back to Turkey.

Education Expenditures: The funds allocated to education are insufficient. 2.3% of the GNP is spent on education. This ratio is 5.4%

EDUCATION EXPENDITURES IN SELECTED COUNTRIES			
Country	(%) of National Income Spent on Education	Country	(%) of National Income Spent on Education
Surinam	9.5	Germany	4.8
Canada	7.2	UK	4.8
Cuba	6.6	South Africa	4.6
USA	6.5	Mexico	4.1
Sweden	6.2	Brazil	3.9
Taiwan	5.9	India	3.8
Portugal	5.7	Pakistan	3.4
Japan	5	Greece	3.1
Kuwait	5	Chile	2.9
Spain	5	Turkey	2.5

for developed countries, 3.9% for underdeveloped countries, and 3.7% for OECD countries. The insufficiency of funds allocated for education becomes clearer when one considers that 21% of Turks are in the 5–14 age group, as compared with 13 in the OECD countries. (Only one country has a population younger than that of Turkey and that is Mexico, with 23% of its population in the 5–14 age group.) Annually, 1.3 million Turkish children reach school age. This number exceeds the total number of children annually reaching school age in Germany, France, and the UK combined. In order to meet the demand for schooling, the government has undertaken major investments. Construction of 480,000 new classrooms was planned for the first decade of the new millennium.

Average monthly salaries for teachers are $295–$390 as compared with around $4000 in developed nations.

GOVERNMENT EXPENDITURES/STUDENT			
Country	Government Expenditures/ Student (US$)	Country	Government Expenditures/ Student (US$)
Canada	1.425	Spain	208
USA	1.272	South Korea	181
Japan	1.111	Hungary	160
France	908	Malaysia	117
Portugal	908	Brazil	86
Germany	832	Turkey	79
Taiwan	344	Mexico	42
Singapore	322	India	34
Chile	208	Pakistan	9

Annual expenditure per student is $200. The same figure is $677 in Italy and $6,593 in the USA. Annual expenditures per student in higher education were $1,711 in 2001 and $1,100 in 2001. The same figure is $6,500 in France, Japan and Germany, $10,000 in Britain, Holland, and France; and $13,000 in the USA. World average for expenditures per student in higher education is $3,370; the EU average is $6,585, and the developed countries average is $5,936.

The government provides free education below the university level. Students in government universities pay approximately 10% of the cost, and scholarships and loans are available. There are private schools at all levels as well. The government subsidizes 45% of the cost of students in private universities. *(World Development Report, 1999;* 2002 *Yili Basinda Egitim (Education at the outset of 2002),* Turkish Ministry of Education.)

Foreign Language Education: The language of instruction is Turkish. At high school level, students can choose to study French, German, or English as a second language. The most popular foreign language taught in schools is English. However, because of the large number of Turkish workers in Germany, German is the most widely spoken foreign language. In special government schools and in most private schools, students spend one preparatory year studying a foreign language and study science and math in that language during their later years.

There are schools that are run by the French, German, American, and Austrian governments or charity institutions. Students in these schools also spend a preparatory year studying a foreign language and later study science and math in that language. Such schools are under the supervision of the Education Ministry, and their curriculums are

like the curriculums of other schools. Foreign schools are a legacy of
the Ottoman Empire. The Lausanne Treaty signed after Turkey's War
of Independence banned the founding of new foreign-run schools but
allowed those already functioning to continue.

Science, Research and Development: According to the figures
of the Science Citation Index (SCI), which keeps a record of scientific
publications worldwide, annual publications by Turkish scientists increased by 460% during the 1987–1997 period. This rate of growth was
exceeded only by South Korea. (During the same period, the publications by US scientists increased by 11%.) The share of Turkish scientists
in world research rose from 0.024% in 1992 to 0.05% in 1998. (Turkey's
population makes up 1% of the world population.)

According to the *Web of Science Database,* in 2001, Turkey was 27th
in terms of scientific articles published. It had been 44th in 1985. Turkish
scientists published 6,393 articles in 2001. During 2001, US scientists
published 246,674 articles, Japanese 72,959, Germans 66,118, British
57,844, French 47,657, Chinese 34,006, Canadians 32,015, Italians 32,176,
Russians 25,233, Australians 20,931, Israelis 10,571, Greeks 5,438, New
Zealanders 4,264, Irish 4,100, South Africans 3,604, Persians 1,511, and
Saudi Arabians 1,361. The increase as compared with the previous year
was 18% in Turkey, as compared with 3.7% worldwide.

In terms of scientific articles per 10,000 persons in the country,
Turkey was 51st in the world in 2000, with a ratio of 0.8. During the
same year, this ratio was 16.85 in Israel, 11.05 in Ireland, 11.01 in New
Zealand, 10.83 in Australia, 9.92 in the UK, 8.68 in the USA, 7.86 in
France, 7.78 in Germany, 5.56 in Japan, 5.25 in Italy, 4.38 in Greece, .8
in South Africa, and 0.61 in Saudi Arabia (*Cumhuriyet Bilim ve Teknik,*
March 17, 2001).

RESEARCH AND DEVELOPMENT EXPENDITURES			
Country	R&D Expenditures as (%) of GNP	Country	R&D Expenditures as (%) of GNP
Japan	2.98	Pakistan	0.98
Germany	2.83	Singapore	0.88
France	2.40	Spain	0.86
Hungary	1.93	Portugal	0.50
USA	1.93	Greece	0.46
South Korea	1.88	Brazil	0.39
Canada	1.37	Turkey	0.31
Italy	1.35	Mexico	0.21

Research and development expenditures are low. In 1999, only 0.63% of national income was spent on R&D (2.9% in South Korea in 1997). 31% of R&D is undertaken by the radio, television, and telecommunications industries. 9% of exports are high technology. Even though Turkey's population is nine times greater than the population of Sweden, the total number of research staff in universities is 13,500 in both Sweden and in Turkey. The number of scientists per million is 209 in Turkey and 2,636 in South Korea. Out of every ten thousand workers, 10.4 in Turkey and 48 in South Korea are employed in R&D. Private companies in Turkey employ 3,634 in R&D; the comparable number is 41,636 in Sweden. The total number of applications for patents is 200 in Turkey and 120,000 in Germany and also in South Korea. Turkey annually earns $160 million through exports of and pays $3.1 billion for the imports of high technology products. (Source: Turkish Technology Development Foundation.)

Computers: Turkey is 33rd among world nations in terms of ownership of personal computers per capita. The total number of personal computers is 1,200,000. This means that there are 2 computers per 100 persons (40 in the USA, 31 in Australia, 30 in Canada, 27 in New Zealand, 25 in the UK, 18 in Israel, 6 in Greece, and 2.5 in South Africa). In 1997, 1 out of every 9 Americans and 1 out of every 20 Israelis bought a new PC, while the ratio for Turkey was 1 out of every 210 (*Hürriyet,* December 6, 1998). Nevertheless, the computer market expanded by 26% in 1997 and by 40% in 1998. Microsoft has recently moved its headquarters for North Africa and the Middle East to Turkey. Illegal duplication of computer programs is a problem. 84% of computers use copied programs, despite heavy penalties.

RELIGION

The Religious Composition of Population: 99.2% of Turks are Moslems, 0.03% are Orthodox Christians, and 0.05% belong to other faiths. 26% of the Turkish Moslems belong to the Alawi sect and the remainder to the Sunni.

Religious Commitment: According to a study conducted by Bogazici University faculty members Binnaz Toprak and Ali Carkoglu (Turkish Economic and Social Studies Foundation, TESEV, 1999), 55% of the population regard themselves as "faithful." 46% of the population performs five daily prayers regularly; 92% fast; and 68% perform the sacrifice ritual. Religious commitment is negatively correlated with income and education.

Religious Tolerance: There is considerable tolerance with respect to the observance of Moslem religious laws and toward other faiths. According to a study by Prof. Binnaz Toprak and Ass. Prof. Ali Carkoglu (TESEV, 1999), 54% of the population define their identity primarily as "a citizen of Turkish Republic," 4% as a "Turk," and 36% as a Moslem. 92% believe that people of different faiths can and should peacefully coexist within same social structure. Even though 59% believe that a Moslem woman should cover her head, 85% believe that a Moslem woman may choose not to cover her head. 86% believe that a Moslem may choose not to pray regularly; 82% believe that a Moslem may choose not to fast; and 67% believe that a Moslem may choose to consume alcohol.

Secularism: Secularism is one of Ataturk's most important reforms. Turkey is one of two truly secular countries in Europe; the other is France. The Turkish State is secular to the extent that official oaths, such as oaths at court, are taken not in the name of God, but in the name of "what the individual regards sacred."

In Turkey, *imams* (Moslem religious professionals) are civic servants. This practice is contradictory to secularism, and yet it is a product of secularism. Ataturk placed *imams* on the government payroll in order to prevent them from developing an independent power base. Foundations set up for the upkeep of mosques during the Ottoman period were nationalized also for the same reason. Currently, the government employs 85,000 persons in jobs related to religion. (As a comparison, the number of elementary school teachers is 225,000.)

Despite the presence of fundamentalist tendencies, the secular principles of Ataturk are firmly in place. According to the Toprak and Carkoglu study (TESEV, 1999), only 21% of population believe that civic laws should be based on Koran. 77% of the population believe that the nation has progressed under the republican government; 67% are opposed to political and state matters being shaped by religion, and 61% are opposed to the existence of political parties based on religious principles.

Even though Ataturk formally introduced it under the Republic, secularism is an ancient tradition and has deep roots with Turks. In Turkey, unlike in other Moslem nations such as Saudi Arabia, the state authority has always been distinct and in a way superior to the religious authority. The Ottoman sultan sought the approval of the Sheik-ul Islam (leader of Islam) for his actions and decrees, yet the absolute power to appoint and remove the Sheik-ul Islam resided with the sultan. The Turkish ruler always retained the right to legislate independently in areas beyond the scope of *sharia* (religious law). As early as 1203, it was stated by an adviser to the Turkish sultan that "the job of the *imam* is to pray and to preach and to leave worldly government in the hands of the sultan." (Prof. Halil Inalcık, Osmanli Imparatorlugu [Ottoman Empire], *Eren Yayincilik,* Istanbul, pp. 319–343.)

Mosque Construction: This moderate attitude toward religion is not reflected in mosque construction, which is conducted with great zeal. Even though Turkey is the only secular Moslem country, the number of mosques in Turkey equals the number of mosques in the other 54 Moslem countries combined. During the Ottoman period, 13,000 mosques were built within the Empire spreading over three continents. Today, the number of mosques is around 73,500, and 1,500 more are being built every year—this in a country where there are 51,000 elementary school and 2,500 high school buildings. There are 2,700 mosque and 2,300 school buildings in Istanbul. The construction of a new mosque starts every six hours, whereas the construction of a new school starts every 10 days. This is despite the fact that mosques are far from being used to capacity. According to a study conducted in 1990, mosques were 1% full for morning, 7% full for noon, 4% full for afternoon, 2% full for evening, and 2% full for night prayer (*Sabah,* April 11, 1990).

Non-Moslems: Turks have traditionally been uniquely tolerant of other religions. Before the Republic was proclaimed, different faiths in the Ottoman Empire lived in what can be called "pluralist equilibrium," even though the sultan, who was the head of the state, was also the caliph, leader of all Moslems in the world. Eastern Christians were safe in their ancient homelands—despite the Crusades and the almost continual hostility with the Christian West. The patriarchate of the Greek Orthodox Church was allowed to stay in Istanbul, and a patriarchate was set up in Istanbul for the Armenian subjects of the sultan. Jews expelled by Catholic kings from Spain and Portugal and those who fled persecution in Central Europe during the Middle Ages were given refuge by the Ottoman rulers. As Monsieur de la Motraye put it, "There is no country on earth where the exercise of all religions is more free and less subject to being troubled, than in Turkey." He knew what he was saying because he was a Huguenot who had been forced to leave France by Louis XIV after 1685. George of Hungary wrote in the fifteenth century, "The Turks do not compel anyone to renounce his faith, do not try hard to persuade anyone, and do not have a great opinion of renegades."

Presently, even though Islam is under state control according to the secular arrangements introduced by Ataturk, other religious communities run their own affairs with regard to matters of religion. Orthodox and Armenian patriarchs remain in Istanbul. There are nearly one hundred churches in Istanbul and several others in the rest of the country. The chief rabbi in Istanbul is the leader of Jewish citizens. In 1992, the Jewish community celebrated the quincentennial anniversary of their arrival in Turkey from Spain; Turkey is the only land where they have lived in peace for 500 years.

Religious Education: Religious education is obligatory beginning in the fourth grade and continuing through high school. The government runs nearly 400 high schools that train *imams* . There are 9 faculties for religious studies and 4 schools of religion affiliated with universities. Mosques run roughly 250 officially certified Koran schools. Private organizations and foundations also run several thousand Koran schools. As of 1996, approximately 17% of all students attending high school were being taught at schools that were also training *imams* . Such schools produced 55,000 graduates annually, even though the annual need for *imams* was only about 2,000. Most graduates of *imam* schools therefore have to seek employment in other fields. Education, law, and civic service are popular vocations among the graduates of *imam* schools.

According to the education reforms of 1997, the primary aim of which was to extend elementary education to eight years, the junior-high-school level of *imam* schools was closed down. These reforms also stipulated that graduates of *imam* schools should continue with their higher education only in the field of religious studies. Following the implementation of these reforms, attendance in *imam* schools dropped drastically, dropping from 476,069 in the 1996–1997 academic year to 356,471 in 1997–1998 and dropping further by 40% in 2000–2001. It is expected that attendance at *imam* schools will drop to 25,000 by 2003. This number will be sufficient to meet the need for new *imams* . Again, in accordance with education reforms of 1997, youth are permitted to attend Koran schools only after completing the first five years of elementary education and only during summer holidays. Following the implementation of this ruling, attendance at Koran schools dropped from 584,966 to 132,420.

Fundamentalism: The religious conservative vote is roughly 15%. Most of the religious conservative vote is a protest vote by those who are disappointed with the decadence and corruption they witness, particularly in large towns. According to a study by Toprak and Assoc. Prof. Carkoglu (TESEV, 1999) 42% believe that the Virtue Party, which defends fundamentalist views, is not "democratic" and 50% believe that this party would turn Turkey into a religious state if it had its way. Virtue and its predecessor Welfare party were closed down by the Constitutional Court, because parties based on religion are against the Constitution. The european Human Rights Court at The Hague upheld the closing of the Welfare Party.

Fundamentalist female college students insist on covering their heads. The Supreme Court has ruled that this behavior is against the constitution, reasoning that since the constitution is secular, religious behavior cannot be allowed in a public institution. Also, female civil servants are not allowed to wear head coverings. A female MP who insisted on wearing her head cover to the assembly meeting hall was not allowed to take her oath. She eventually lost her citizenship and seat since it turned out that she had applied for and acquired US citizenship and not informed the Turkish government beforehand, as the law requires. Three quarters of those polled in the Toprak and Carkoglu study believe that female students and civil servants should be able to cover their heads, if they should so wish. According to the same study, 42% believe that secular authorities repress believers and 31% believe that they cannot practice religion as they wish.

LAW

Legal System: Independent boards affiliated with the Justice Ministry oversee appointments of prosecutors and judges. The appeals courts are in Ankara. If a lower court insists on a ruling overruled by an appeals court, the combined body of all appeals courts hears the case. The decision of this body is final. There is a constitutional court that determines whether laws and decrees are in accordance with the constitution. Separate independent judicial authorities supervise government appointments and expenditures. Lower-court cases are decided on by a single judge and higher-court cases by three judges. Penalties are low, with the exception of penalties against organized crime and armed robberies. Well-behaved convicts serve only one third of their terms. There is the death penalty for premeditated murder and for armed organized uprising against the state. However, the death penalty needs to be approved by the parliament and by the president as if it were a law. The parliament has refused to debate any death sentences for the past twenty years, effectively turning death sentences into life imprisonment.

Crime Rate: For a rapidly industrializing country with a high population growth and urbanization rate, the crime rate remains astonishingly low. Incarceration rate (number imprisoned per 100,000) is roughly 100. Incarceration rate is 40 in Japan, 90 in Italy and France, 95 in Germany, 110 in Canada, 125 in the UK, and 680 in the USA *(Monthly Review,* July/August 2001).

36

CRIME RATE (PER 1000 PERSONS)	
Country	Crime Rate (per 1000 persons)
UK	102
Canada	100
Germany	71
France	68
USA	54
Switzerland	51
Italy	38
Greece	29
Turkey	3.6

Source: UN and Interpol Statistics, Anadolu Agency, July 4, 2000

Crime in Istanbul: The crime rate in Istanbul is relatively low compared with other large world metropolises. The population of Istanbul is equal to the population of Athens, Rome, and Berlin combined. Yet, the total number of crimes committed in Istanbul is only half as much as the total number of crimes committed in these three cities combined. In 1997 the total number of crimes committed was 126,000 in Istanbul, 595,000 in Berlin, 276,000 in Paris, 248,000 in Tokyo, 215,000 in Rome, and 162,000 in Vienna. 36.1% of all crime in Turkey is committed in Istanbul. Crimes committed in Istanbul dropped by 14% in 2000, as compared with 1999.

The city has 18,850 police officers, 10,000 lawyers, and 300,000 ex-convicts. There are 30,000 parking spaces in town, whereas 600,000 are needed. There is only one policeman per 1,000 vehicles.

COMMON FELONIES	
Felony	% of those who Entered Prison Convicted for this Felony
Against property	18
Against individuals	14
Against public decency and family	8
Against public security and welfare	4

Drug Trafficking: Turkey is at the crossroads of major international drug-transportation routes. Opium and hashish from the East goes to the West via Turkey, and drugs such as Ecstasy and Coptagon are transported via Turkey to the East. The government wages a strong campaign against illicit drug trafficking. During the 1990s, about 10% of world drug traffic took place through Turkey. In 1998, 60% of all drugs captured in Europe and 40% of those captured in the world were captured in Turkey. Since 1999, drug trafficking has shifted to other routes. Two alternate routes that have gained importance are from Central Asia through Russia and from Myanmar across the Indian Ocean through Nigeria. (*Aktüel*, 509, 2001.)

CRIME IN ISTANBUL AND IN SELECTED MAJOR CITIES						
Year	City	Murder	Theft	Car Theft	Mugging	Rape
1990	Istanbul	241	647	2744	458	N/A
	London	188	188,000	80,000	38,000	N/A.
1991	NYC	2,202	N/A	N/A	126,119	3062
	LA	1,856	N/A	N/A	129,124	4114
	Chicago	1,027	N/A	N/A	77,623	4403
	Houston	608	N/A	N/A	10,947	1213
	Dallas	500	N/A	N/A	13,449	1208
1992	Istanbul	311	11681	41	747	3307
	Moscow	1,238	37,004	10,680	N/A	362
1995	Istanbul	313	10,983	5,898	766	N/A
	Tokyo	121	219,374	2,116	548	157
	Moscow	1,238	37,004	10,680	4,986	362
	Paris	130	233,205	29,768	69,162	2306

Source: Istanbul Police Headquarters; *Milliyet*, December 2, 1991; *Hürriyet*, January 7, 1992

LIFE STYLE

The Wedding Ceremony: Marriage is usually preceded by a proposal visit by the bridegroom and his family to the bride's home. After this visit, the bride and the bridegroom are considered as being "promised to each other." If the bride and the bridegroom continue to like each other after they are "promised," they become "engaged" and put on "engagement rings" at an "engagement party" held among relatives and close friends. At this party, it is customary for an elderly and respected relative to present the bride and the bridegroom their rings. The "engagement" ring is worn on the right hand. Rings are switched to left hands after the wedding. "Engagement" brings no legal obligations. However, in more traditional areas, the reputation of a girl can be damaged by the breakup of an "engagement."

The wedding is held a few months after the engagement. Before the wedding, families of the bride and the bridegroom buy furniture for the house of the young couple. Usually, the bride's family buys the bedroom furniture and the kitchen utilities, and the bridegroom's family buys the living room furniture and appliances such as a washing machine and a vacuum cleaner. Dowry payments are rare. Jewelry and gold is presented to the bride at the wedding, and these remain her property even if there is a divorce. This custom can be considered a form of financial security for the wife and mother-to-be.

Marriage ceremonies take place in civic halls. The mayor or his or her representative carries out the wedding ceremony in the presence of two witnesses. Relatives and friends attend. It is customary to send wreaths to the wedding. As they leave, guests are presented sugarcoated almonds or other candies in nicely decorated little packs. A party can be given in the evening. The newlyweds usually leave for a honeymoon after the party.

Both men and women attend wedding parties in large cities. In the countryside, separate wedding parties are held for men and women. Female guests meet in the home of the bride, and male guests meet in the home of the bridegroom. Women dye their fingers with a red paint called *kina* (henna) and perform local dances themselves. (According to Piar-Gallup, such an evening is organized at 83.9% of weddings. *Cumhuriyet*, June 10, 1998.) Men drink, watch performances by local artists, and, in some cases, fire their guns. Festivities in both houses usually last all night. The following day, the bridegroom's family takes the bride from her natal home. In the country, the newlyweds usually live in the bridegroom's family home for some time. In urban areas, the newlyweds usually move directly to their own homes if they can afford to do so.

Moslem Feasts: There are two major religious festivals in Islam. One comes at the end of the month of Ramadan, and the other two months later. The first lasts for three days and the second lasts for four days. During the first feast, the ending of Ramadan is celebrated. During the second, a pilgrimage is carried out to the Kabba in Mecca, and those who can afford to, offer rams as sacrifice. During Moslem holidays, new dresses are bought for children. People visit the homes of elderly relatives and friends.

Moslem Rituals: Moslem believers practice the following five rituals:

1. To testify that there is only one God, Allah, and that Mohammad is his servant and prophet.

2. To pray five times (morning, noon, afternoon, evening, and night, times being determined by the position of the sun) every day.

3. To fast from sunrise till sunset every day during the month of Ramadan. Moslem months are based on a lunar calendar. The Moslem calendar starts at 622 AD, the year the Prophet Mohammad migrated from Mecca to Medina. Therefore, the time of Ramadan according to the Western calendar varies every year.

4. To conduct a pilgrimage to the Kabba in Mecca.

5. To pay 2.5% of one's annual income as alms to the poor. Alms are to be paid not to the mosque or to a religious organization but directly to the needy, beginning with one's immediate relatives.

Daily Prayers: Prayer times are announced by the *muezzin*, who chants, in Arabic the holy *ezan*, (call to prayer) from the balcony of the minaret: "Allah is the Greatest, Mohammad is his servant and his prophet, come to happiness, come to salvation". Nowadays, one rarely sees a *muezzin* on the balcony of a minaret. Loudspeakers and cassette players are used instead. Prayers can be performed at any time between the beginning of one prayer and start of the next one. It is possible to later make up for a prayer that a believer missed due to a binding obligation. One can pray wherever he or she is since one is in the presence of Allah at all times and places. However, it is better to pray in mosques with other believers. It is necessary to make ablutions before prayers, so ablution fountains are found next to most mosques. In mosques, the *imam* leads the prayer immediately after the *ezan*. The *imam* does not mediate between the believers and god as priests do in some other religions. Rather, the *imam* simply leads the prayer, and everybody repeats his actions.

During prayers, members of the congregation line up in rows behind the *imam*. All believers are equal when praying. Therefore, there is no stratification in mosques and those who come earlier get to pray in the front rows. It is believed that angels record the male believers beginning at the front row and the female believers beginning at the back row. This is the reason why, at prayer times, men are seen rushing to join the front row and why women pray at the back or on the balconies.

In Turkish, two words of Arabic origin are used to refer to a "mosque:" *masjit* and *jamii*. Masjit is a small mosque; *jamii* is a larger mosque where Friday speeches can be given. The word "mosque" is derived from *masjit*. In Arabic, *masjit* means "a place to prostrate one-self" and *jamii* means "Friday." Both the *jamii* and the *masjit* are built to face Mecca. Inside, at the center of the wall facing Mecca, there is the *mihrab* where the *imam* prays. The *jamii* also has a pulpit, called the *minbar*, from which the sermon is delivered before the noon prayer on Friday.

The Friday sermon has a secular as well as a religious function because it marks the sovereignty of the state. The sermon is given on behalf of the sovereign. In Turkey it is on behalf of the Turkish Republic. During the early days of Islam, Friday speeches were given by leading members of the community. In Turkey, Friday sermons are delivered by the appointed *imam* of the mosque or by a religious official who has been appointed specifically for this task. The state religious organization recommends to the speakers the topics to be covered at the sermons.

Funeral Ceremonies: The deceased is washed and wrapped in a white shroud. A plain wooden coffin is used for burial. The body of the deceased is not put on display for friends and relatives. The funeral ceremony can be carried out at the end of any one of the daily prayers. For convenience, usually the noon or the afternoon prayer is chosen.

The ceremony can be carried out at the end of the first prayer following the death. However, it is customary to wait at least a day in order for faraway relatives and friends to join the ceremony. Members of both sexes attend a funeral ceremony. In the past, even if the deceased was a female, only men attended the actual funeral prayers, which are brief, lasting no more than a few minutes. Now however, women participate in this phase of the funeral ceremony as well. Even though there is no such requirement, funeral prayers are by convention held in the mosque courtyard.

Following the prayers, the *imam* asks the congregation members their opinion of the deceased. They all answer that they knew him or her as a very good person. It is a sin to express negative opinions about the dead. Then the *imam* asks whether they will testify to this at the final judgment day. The congregation answers loudly, "Yes!" Following this ceremony, the coffin is carried off.

The custom is to carry the coffin on the shoulders. A hearse is used if the graveyard is not within walking distance. However, it is customary to carry the coffin on the shoulders at least on the way to the hearse and from the hearse to the grave. Because carrying a coffin is believed to be a good deed, men rush to do so.

Only men carry the coffin. Women stay at the back of the funeral procession. Men bring the coffin to the grave as the women watch from a distance. The body, wrapped in a white shroud, is taken out of the coffin before burial. Close male relatives enter the grave pit in order to help to lower the body. Again, to shovel earth into the grave is believed to be a good deed, and men rush to use the spades in order to fill up the grave. Following the burial, the *imam* who has led the ceremony has a solitary moment of prayer by the grave.

Strictly speaking, Islam does not allow grave visits. In Saudi Arabia, where this rule is followed, even the kings do not have graves: a piece of stone in the desert marks the grave of a Saudi king. According to the Koran, it is a sin to request things from the dead. When praying for his or her dead, one should only pray for God's mercy for him or her. In Turkey, graves of persons raised to the status of saints by folk belief are frequented by those who make wishes from them, ignoring the explicit ban of Islam.

Tea and Coffee Consumption: Contrary to what one might expect, Turkey is a land of tea drinkers, not coffee drinkers. "Turkish coffee" is famous worldwide and coffee was introduced to the world by way of Turkey. However, coffee is not grown in Turkey and never was. "Turkish coffee" is the name given to a way of making coffee. Coffee is native to Ethiopia and was introduced to Yemen during the fifteenth century and to Istanbul, capital of the Ottoman Empire, by the governor of Yemen during the sixteenth century. Sacks of coffee were among the materials left behind by the retreating Ottoman army after the failure of the 1683 siege of Vienna, and a captured Turkish Janissary soldier introduced the Viennese to the art of coffee making.

ANNUAL PER CAPITA COFFEE CONSUMPTION (KG)			
Country	Annual per Capita Coffee Consumption	Country	Annual per Capita Coffee Consumption
Finland	11.6	France	6.0
Sweden	11.3	USA	4.5
Austria	10.3	Italy	4.4
Holland	10.0	Japan	2.9
Switzerland	8.7	England	2.4
Germany	7.5	Turkey	0.1

The total annual consumption of tea is 120,000 tons. Turkish tea is grown along the Black Sea coast in the province of Rize. The annual consumption of coffee is 8,000 tons, 6,000 of which is prepared as Turkish coffee; the rest is instant or filtered. On the average, a Turk consumes 27 cups of coffee annually, whereas a Dutch person consumes 2,000 cups. The annual per-capita coffee consumption is only 100 grams.

Making Turkish Tea and Coffee: Turkish tea is made by simmering the tea leaves in a small pot over a larger pot of boiling water. Some of the hot water is added and the pot is allowed to continue to simmer. The tea is served in small, thin glasses. Dark tea from the small pot and boiling water is mixed in the glass according to taste.

When making Turkish coffee, finely ground coffee and water and the desired amount of sugar are heated in a small pot. The pot is taken off the fire after a foam forms but before it actually boils. Coffee is served in small cups. The silt at the bottom is not consumed. It is believed that the remaining residue found at the bottom of the cooled cup can reveal your fortune.

Consumption of Alcoholic Beverages: In Turkey, the sale and consumption of alcoholic beverages is not banned as required by Islam. 3.2% of the GNP is spent on alcoholic beverages and cigarettes. The annual per capita alcohol consumption is 18 liters, compared with 21 liters in the USA and 19 liters in Germany. 25% of the population are alcohol users. 12.5% of the adult population over twenty-five are alcoholics of various degrees. The consumption of alcoholic beverages increased by 900% between 1982 and 1990. 800 million bottles of alcoholic beverages are consumed annually.

Annual wine production is about 60 million liters. Per-capita wine consumption is 1 liter in Turkey, compared with 59 in France, 54 in Italy, 30 in Greece, 9 in South Africa, and 8 in the USA. Annual beer consumption is 824 million liters (roughly 12 liters per capita). The Efes group controls 80% of the market for beer. (Sources: State Institute of Statistics, Turkish Green Crescent Society.)

Raki: The most popular alcoholic beverage is *raki,* the Turkish equivalent of the Mediterranean liquor, known as Ricard or Pernod (or the notorious *pastis)* in France, as *ouzo* in Greece, and as *arak* in Arab countries. *Raki* represents 72% of all alcohol consumed annually. Annual *raki* consumption was 67 million liters in 2000, or 1.5 liters per adult. *Raki* consumption has been dropping steadily from the peak of 74 million liters in 1998, primarily because of competition from cheap imports of whisky. *Raki* is made by mixing aniseed with alcohol distilled from dried grapes in traditional copper barrels that can hold up to 5,000 liters each. *(Arak* is distilled from dates, and *ouzo* is distilled from mastic.) Since 1920s, all *raki* has been produced by the Turkish State Monopoly. Kulüp and Altinbas brands contain 50% alcohol; the more popular Yeni Raki brand contains 45%. The drink is served in tall, thin glasses and is usually diluted with two-thirds water. A second glass of water helps to clear the palate. *Meze* dishes (appetizers) such as feta cheese, melon, aubergine purée, salted fish, and various salads usually accompany *raki.* According to the nineteenth-century poet and *raki* connoisseur Ahmet Rasim, the first glass should be consumed fast in order to attain a "pleasant frame of mind"; the subsequent glasses should be consumed more slowly in order to obtain maximum relaxation and enjoyment of company. Tripe *(iskembe)* soup, served by late night (i.e. early-morning) specialty shops, is generally accepted as the only known antidote for a *raki* hangover.

Cigarette Consumption: After Greece, Turkey has the second highest per-capita cigarette consumption rate in Europe. One out of three adults and half of adult males smoke. The tendency to smoke is rising among youth, mainly because role models such as mothers, fathers, teachers, doctors, and well-known actors and actresses tend to be smokers. Annually, 100,000 persons die due to problems related to smoking. The average age for those with coronary problems is 56 for men and 64 for women. These averages are ten years younger than in the West. (Study by Coronary Thrombosis Club, Istanbul.) Among European countries, Turkey has the highest percentage of coronary diseases in the adult (45–74 age group) female population and the third highest percentage in the adult male population. (Turkish Cardiology Society, *Hürriyet,* December 8, 2001.) A health warning is mandatory on cigarettes, and cigarette advertising is not allowed. It is estimated that the 10% tax on tobacco discourages only 10% of smokers.

The Turkish Language: The Turkish language belongs to the Altaic branch of the Ural-Altaic family of languages and thus is closely related to Mongolian, Korean, Japanese, Finnish, and Hungarian. The fundamental features that distinguish the Ural-Altaic languages from the Indo-European are:

1. Vowel harmony,

2. Absence of gender,

3. Agglutination,

4. Adjectives preceding nouns, and

5. Verbs coming at the end of the sentence.

Turkish is the sixth most widely spoken language in the world. Turkish dialects include Azeri, Turkoman, Tartar, Uzbek, Baskurti, Nogay, Kyrgyz, Cossack, Yakuti, Cuvas, and several other dialects, all of which go back to a common Ur-Altaic. The language spoken in Turkey proper is one of the southwestern dialects of the Western Turkish language family.

Recent studies show that Turkish is 8,500 years old and possibly related to ancient Sumerian. (The word for "day" is *gün* in Turkish and *kun* in Sumerian; the word for "person" is *kishi* in Turkish and *giish* in Sumerian; the word for "arm" is *kol* in Turkish and *kuullah* in Sumerian; and the word for "god" is *tanrı* in Turkish and *dengri* in Sumerian.)

Leisure Activities: According to a recent Piar-Gallup poll (*Radikal,* June 9, 1998 and *Cumhuriyet,* June 10, 1998), 90.8% of Turks do not belong to clubs or societies; 1.2% are sports club members. 5.8% go to the cinema, 3.4% go to the theatre, and 2.3% go to ballet and opera performances. 3.2% exercise regularly; 23% exercise occasionally. 72.5% do not watch live sports events, and 52.6% do not watch sports events on TV. 44.9% do not read books. 65.9% do not go on vacation, and 11.7% go on vacation only once a year.

44

GROWTH AND INCOME DISTRIBUTION

Economic Performance: Turkish economy is experiencing grave economic difficulties at the beginning of the new millennium. Following –6.4% economic growth in 1999, the economy had bounced back with 6.4% growth in 2000. But –8% growth was experienced in 2001.

The difficulties followed a period of bright performance during the previous decade. In 1998, Turkey's GNP of $200.5 billion, was the 22nd largest in the world. The GNP had increased 12.7 times since 1970. During 1965–1994, Turkey had the highest GNP growth rate among developing nations. GNP growth had averaged 4.3% over 1965–1998, which made Turkey the 7th fastest-growing economy in the world, together with Japan and Brazil (China 8.6%, South Korea 8.1%, Thailand 7.3%, Indonesia 6.8%, Saudi Arabia 5.4%, and India 4.9%). The GNP growth rate was 5.1% over 1980–1997 (2.7% in the UK, 2.6% in Spain, 2.3% in Holland and Portugal, 2% in France and Austria, 1.9% in Italy and 1.5% in Greece).

DISTRIBUTION OF GNP BETWEEN SECTORS (%)		
Sector	% Share of Sector Output in Total GNP	% of Working Force in the Sector
Agriculture	16	45
Industry	31	20
Trade	17	4
Other Services	36	31

The per-capita GNP increased by 4.9% during 1990–1999. This performance is quite impressive, particularly if one considers that only 33 countries achieved sustained 3% or more annual growth in per-capita GNP during 1980–96. For 59 countries, mainly in sub-Saharan Africa and the countries of the former Eastern Bloc, per capita declined during this period.

GNP INCREASES IN SELECTED COUNTRIES			
Country	GNP in 1970(billion $)(2)	GNP in 1993 (billion $)(3)	Increase (3)/(2)
South Korea	9	331	36
Saudi Arabia	5	122	24
Thailand	7	125	17
Indonesia	10	145	15

However, Turkey's recent economic performance was not as impressive as the performance of certain other fast-growing countries. In 1950, Turkey's per-capita GNP was one fifth of the per-capita GNP in Western Europe. Today, the same ratio is one twelfth. During the previous decade, when Turkey's GNP grew annually at the average rate of 4.9%, the per-capita GNP of Greece doubled. In 1980, per-capita income was approximately the same in South Korea and Turkey: $1,520 in South Korea and $1,470 in Turkey. As of 1997, per capita in South Korea was about five times as much as per capita in Turkey.

Recent economic woes have been attributed to the earthquake in 1999 and to a dispute between the president and the prime minister, which took place at the beginning of 2001. Yet even though these incidents may have triggered the economic problems, true reasons for the crisis are rooted much deeper.

It is the opinion of this author that at the root of Turkey' current economic ills lies the industrialization-under-protection strategy adopted in the 1960s. High-cost products produced by the inefficient industries under protection could only be consumed by stimulating domestic demand. This is the essential cause behind the large budget deficits the country has witnessed since the late 1960s. Military expenditures necessitated by the struggle against the PKK insurgency and expenditures on the massive energy and irrigation projects in southeast Turkey further worsened the situation. An inefficient taxation system, the social security system, which enabled workers to retire after only twenty-five years of work, losses by government-owned firms, employment of too many in government jobs, and wasteful government spending in general were the other factors that contributed to government deficits.

Domestic and international borrowing financed the deficits. Beginning in the 1990s, restrictions on international capital movements were completely lifted and borrowing became more reckless. Real returns on borrowing by the Turkish government rose to be as high as 25% per year. As debt multiplied rapidly, it was quite clear that it was only a matter of time before this state of affairs would lead to a major bottleneck and crisis.

At the end of 2001, the IMF came to the rescue of the Turkish economy with a massive loan of $31 billion, an amount that was equal to the debt service of the nation during that year. Whereas this loan secured the debt service of Turkey's creditors in the immediate future, it was not so clear whether, together with the economic policies dictated by the IMF, it would help to solve Turkey's economic problems. The influx of dollars with the IMF loan lowered the exchange rate and

46

reduced the competitiveness of the Turkish economy. Heavy taxation demanded by the IMF stifled internal demand. In the medium range, the Turkish economy is likely to do better as industry improves its competitiveness, following customs union with the EU, and as tourism recovers from the blows it received after September 11 and the events in the Middle East. In the long run, Turkey's hopes for economic prosperity lies in EU membership, in the manner that Greece, Ireland, Spain, and Portugal achieved prosperity.

PER CAPITA GNP IN SELECTED COUNTRIES (1998)			
Country	per capita GNP	Country	per capita GNP
Switzerland	40,080	Spain	14,080
Japan	32,380	Greece	11,650
USA	29,340	South Korea	7,970
Germany	25,850	Brazil	4,570
France	24,940	Turkey	3,247
Kuwait	22,110	South Africa	2,880
UK	21,400	Russia	2,300
Australia	20,540	Iran	1,770
Italy	20,250	Romania	1,390
Canada	20,020	Egypt	1,290
New Zealand	14,700	Bulgaria	1,230

Development Indices: Per-capita GNP was estimated as $2,160 in 2001, down from $3,247 in 1998. Per-capita GNP is higher in real terms. When differences in purchasing power were taken into consideration, Turkey's national per-capita income was estimated as $6,986 in 2000. (State Planning Organization, *Economic Program for 2002.*)

Another measure of welfare, the "Human Development Index" (HDI), developed by the United Nations Development Program (UNDP), takes indicators such as life expectancy and the education level of the population into consideration as well as national income of the population in order to measure welfare. In 1999, Turkey was 99th among 174 countries in terms of HDI. Turkey had the seventh-highest HDI growth rate during the years 1970–1990.

Non-Recorded Economic Activities: A number of economic activities are not recorded because of tax evasion and other reasons, and therefore do not enter into national income accounts. Non-recorded economic activities consist of "informal," "underground," and "criminal" activities. Production of food for domestic consumption is among many other innocent "informal" economic activities included under this heading.

HUMAN DEVELOPMENT INDICES (1999)			
Country	HDI	Country	HDI
Canada	0.982	Romania	0.752
USA	0.927	Russia	0.747
Japan	0.924	Saudi Arabia	0.740
Australia	0.922	Brazil	0.739
UK	0.918	Turkey	0.728
France	0.918	Armenia	0.728
Germany	0.906	Jordan	0.715
New Zealand	0.901	Iran	0.715
Italy	0.900	South Africa	0.695
Israel	0.883	Syria	0.663
Greece	0.867	Egypt	0.616
Bulgaria	0.758	Iraq	0.586

It is estimated that 4–4.5 million are employed in non-recorded activities. The total volume of such economic activity is estimated to be 40–50% (*Hürriyet*, July 20, 2001) of the official or "recorded" economy (45% in Poland, 24% in Italy, 15% in France, 15% in Germany and the USA, 12% in UK, 9% in Japan, and 6% in Switzerland).

When the "underground" economy is taken into consideration, per-capita income in Turkey is probably higher than the official figure by 40% (Dr. Turkmen Derdiyok, in his "Estimate of Turkey's Unofficial Economy," *Milliyet* June 6, 1993). According to the Director of the State Institute of Statistics, Prof. Dr. Omer Gebizlioglu, when the "underground" economy is taken into consideration, per-capita income in Turkey was $11,000 in 1998 (*Hürriyet*, June 9, 1998).

Income Distribution: According to the *Development Indices* published by the World Bank in 2000, Turkey was 70th amongst nations on the Gini Index, a measure for the equality of income distribution. In this respect, Turkey is in the same category as the USA: The Gini Index is 41.5 for Turkey and 40.8 for the USA.

INCOME DISTRIBUTION FOR URBAN AND RURAL HOUSEHOLDS				
Percentage of Households	Urban 1992	Urban 1999	Rural 1992	Rural 1999
Lowest 20%	5.4	4.8	5.2	5.6
Fourth 20%	9.3	8.2	10.1	10
Third 20%	13.6	11.9	14.8	15
Second 20%	20.7	17.9	21.8	22
Top 20%	50.9	57.2	47.7	47.8

The top 20% of Turkey's population receive 55% of the national income and the lowest 20% receive only 5%. The income gap between the richest fifth and the poorest fifth is estimated as 8 for rural and as 12 for urban households. The same ratio is 5 for the EU countries and 74 for the world as a whole (30 in 1960). The per-capita income of the lowest 20% of the population is estimated around $537 (below the $690 poverty line of the UN) and the per-capita income of the top 20% of the population is estimated around $ 6,019. The per-capita income of the top 5% (3.5 million persons) is $19,329, whereas the per-capita income of those in the lowest 5% group is $400. There are 2,500 Dollar millionaires in Turkey.

According to another study, the richest 3 million, who make up 4.5% of the population, receive 25% of the GNP; and the poorest, who make up 12 million or 17.5% of the population, receive 6%. The per-capita income of the richest 4.5% is $16,000 and of the poorest 17.5% $500. On the average, the richest 600,000 families spend $4,650 every month, and the poorest 2,400,000 spend $150 (Gungor Uras, on the basis of findings of Ac Nielsen Zet, *Milliyet* May 22, 2001).

1% of the population in Istanbul captures 30% of the GNP produced in this town. In 2000, 0.3% of urban population had per-capita income over $32,000. 75% of urban population had per capita income below $2000, and 20.4% below $481 (*Milliyet* April 23, 2001). Average annual income for urban households is $7,753. This figure is $9,717 for the households in larger metropolitan cities such as Istanbul and $6,213 for the households in smaller cities. The average income of 80% of the families in smaller cities and 60% of those in metropolitan cities is below the national average. 85% of urban disposable income is controlled by 40% of urban households. Income of the top 10% of urban households equals the income of 45% of the urban households that make up the low-income group (VERI ARASTIRMA A.S., *Kentsel Turkiye Raporu, Report on Urban Turkey*).

Wage earners earn 25% of GNP; recipients of rent, interest, and profits earn 58%. Those who are employed in agriculture earn three times less than those who are employed in industry.

Regional Income Distribution: There is inequality of income between regions as well. Per-capita income in the east is about one third of national average (*Sabah*, August 19, 1989). Istanbul captures 27.5% of the GNP and Istanbul, Ankara, and Izmir together capture 37%. The average household income in Istanbul ($11,367) is three times the national average.

INCOME DISTRIBUTION BETWEEN REGIONS		
Region	Households Living in the Region (%)	Share of GNP (%)
Marmara (Istanbul And Environs)	26.6	38.6
Aegean (Western Turkey)	15.7	13.9
Mediterranean (Southwest)	12.5	11.0
Central Turkey	17.9	15.4
Black Sea	12.8	10.9
East	7.1	5.7
Southeast	7.4	4.5

INFLATION AND PRIVATIZATION

Inflation: Turkey has been a high-inflation country for the past 25 years. Prices increased by 21,544% during the previous decade. The inflation rate for 1999 was 68%, the ninth highest in the world. The country managed to survive successfully with inflation mainly because the exchange rate was allowed to fluctuate and because real wages were flexible. In the past, whenever the inflation rate rose too high, the exchange rate depreciated and real wages fell.

In December 1999, the Turkish Government signed a stand-by agreement with the IMF with the intention of bringing inflation under control. Under the terms of this agreement, wage and price increases and currency depreciation rate were to be limited to 20%. The arrangements fell apart with the crisis in February 2001, when the exchange rate depreciated by 100%. In the aftermath, the exchange rate was allowed to fluctuate. During 2001, the wholesale price index rose by 88.6% and the consumer price index rose by 68.5%.

Persistent large budget deficits, which were roughly equal to 25% of the budget in the very recent past and rose to 44% in 2001, are the main reasons for the high rate of inflation. Budget deficits are caused by:

1. Subsidies for state-owned economic enterprises,

2. Social-security subsidies,

3. Insufficient taxation, and

4. Service on the previously accumulated debt.

Problems related to social security, insufficient taxation, and debt service have been discussed earlier in this book. A few words are said below about state-owned economic enterprises and their privatization.

Privatization: State-owned economic enterprises are a legacy of the early years of the Republic, when industrialization was undertaken by the state in an effort to make up for the shortage of capital created by the Great Depression. Textile, steel, cement, glass, paper, sugar industries, production of energy, oil and other minerals, railways, airlines, and shipping enterprises were undertaken by the state. These enterprises served a valuable purpose in promoting industrialization and in training workers and managers. Today, subsidies to the enterprises employing old technology and too many workers are a burden on the government budget. Efforts are under way for privatization in order to improve efficiency and technology.

In 1983 Turkey was one of the first countries to start a privatization program. But the rate of progress of privatization has been rather slow. Nevertheless, $3.165 billion worth of privatization was realized between 1990–1996, making Turkey the third in this area after Hungary ($10.185 billion) and Poland ($3.599 billion). In 1998, major progress seemed to be under way with the sales of public shares in the Is Bankasi, one of the largest banks in Turkey, and of the state-owned oil company POAS. However, the down payment from the sale of POAS failed to materialize. Privatization efforts were dealt a further blow when serious accusations of corruption were brought in relation to the sale of Turkbank. Privatization, which remained around 50 million dollars in 1999, gained speed in 2000. A total of $4.9 billion was obtained through the sales of the oil company POAS ($1.26 billion), the oil refinery TUPRAS ($1.125 billion), and the sale of the new GSM network ($2.525 billion). With these sales, total volume of privatization realized had exceeded $10 billion by 2001.

INDUSTRY, ENERGY, AND OIL

Industrial Production: Turkey is self sufficient in the production of paper, sugar, glass, cement, steel, and glass. Cars, busses, and trucks, and all household goods such as radios, television sets, videos, washing machines, and vacuum cleaners are assembled in Turkey. There are three major steel mills, five refineries, and two petrochemical complexes. Turkey is the twelfth-largest producer of steel in the world, the sixth-largest producer of cement, the fourth-largest producer of cotton fiber, the sixth-largest producer of cotton yarn, and the fourth-largest producer of woolen fibers.

Textiles, garments, other woven goods, and leather goods account for 25% of manufacturing output and 30% of manufacturing employment. Capacity is 2.5 times the domestic demand, and the industry is therefore export-oriented. Recently, the industry has been challenged by competition from the Far East. However Turkey has a long tradition in the field and much skilled labor. In order to meet the challenge, the textile industry is likely to concentrate more on finished and high-value fabrics, ready-to-wear garments, and high-quality, branded designs.

Presently, Turkey's annual motor-vehicle production capacity is 690,000. This figure can be raised to 1,200,000. 0.6% of world car production is realized in Turkey. Renault, Fiat, Ford, Toyota, Honda, and Hyundai are the car producers. Mercedes Benz is the largest producer of busses and Chrysler the largest producer of trucks. 40% of production capacity is controlled by Fiat, 26% by Renault, and 16% by Toyota. In 2000, Renault produced half of all cars sold in Turkey and Fiat produced 30%. Ford, in cooperation with the Turkish conglomerate Koc (which owns half of Turkish Fiat as well), recently completed the construction of a $400 million plant in Izmit. This new Ford facility will produce 150,000 vehicles annually. Two-thirds of the production will be commercial vehicles. 95% of the output will be exported. On the average, 70% of the parts of the vehicles produced in Turkey are Turkish made. During the first eight months of 2001, automotive production dropped by 31% as compared with the same period the previous year. This was mainly due to the 35% drop in domestic sales. Exports, however, rose by 116%. Automotive exports rose by a further 7% during the first half of 2002, as compared with the previous year. 23% of automotive exports go to Germany.

Turkey is the biggest producer of TV sets in Europe after the UK. Turkish producers control 25% of the TV market in Europe. Total annual production was 9 million sets in 1999. A major producer of household goods is Arcelik, which exports its products to Europe under the brand name Beko.

Energy Sources: Energy consumption per capita is 1.2 ton oil equivalent (TOE). The major sources of energy are oil (43%), coal (28%), natural gas (15%), hydro-energy (4%), and others (10%). "Others" include wood and animal waste, which are used as sources of energy primarily in the countryside. Turkey's primary energy consumption will be about 169 million TOE in 2010. Turkey's energy sources in 2010 will be coal (34%), oil (28%), natural gas (30%), hydro energy (4%), and other sources (4%). Only 12% of hydro potential is utilized. Annual coal production (hard and lignite) is about 55 million tons. 65% of energy needs is imported. This ratio will rise to 72% in 2010.

Oil and the Baku-Tbilisi-Ceyhan Pipeline: Annual oil production is 3 million tons and remaining known reserves are 27 million tons. Domestic production meets 10% of consumption, which was 31.9 tons in 1999. Oil demand will rise to 45 million tons in 2010 and to 64 million tons in 2020. During 1979–84, when oil prices were high, payments for oil imports were equal to 32–40% of total imports. Following the decline of oil prices, the share of oil imports in the total volume of imports declined to 17%. Saudi Arabia (68%) and United Arab Emirates (13%) are the largest suppliers of oil to Turkey.

Detailed engineering studies were commissioned on May 15, 2001, for the Baku-Tbilisi-Ceyhan pipeline, which will bring oil from the Chirali-Gunesli fields of Azarbeijan to the southern Turkish port of Ceyhan on the Mediterranean. The Azerbeijani oil consortium AIOC will finance the $2.4 billion pipeline. The government-owned Turkish oil company TPAO has a 6.75% stake in AIOC, which was formed by eleven companies from the US, Norway, Japan, Saudi Arabia, England, Russia, Scotland, and Azerbaijan. The Turkish Company BOTAS will contract part of the pipeline within Turkish borders and the terminal at Ceyhan. The Turkish government has guaranteed to pay the extra expenses if the costs of production within Turkey should exceed the estimated $1.3 billion.

The Baku-Tbilisi-Ceyhan pipeline is expected to reach Turkey by 2005. 50 million tons of crude oil will be transported on the pipeline to Ceyhan. Turkey's annual revenue from the pipeline will be up to 300 million dollars in rent and in maintenance fees. Initial flow will be one million barrels a day. This amount will be doubled in a decade. Part of the produce from the Tenghiz and Kashagan fields of Kazakhstan will also be diverted to the new pipeline. This will help to relieve pressure on the straits, an additional benefit for Turkey.

Natural Gas and "Blue Stream" Pipeline: Natural gas is used for domestic needs in several large cities and increasingly in power stations. Consumption of natural gas was 13 billion cubic meters in 2000 and will rise to 55 billion cubic meters in 2010 and to 83 billion cubic meters in 2020. Production of natural gas is 99 million cubic meters; remaining recoverable reserves are 10.2 billion cubic meters. 60% of natural gas needs are met through imports from the Soviet Union via a pipeline through Romania and Bulgaria. Liquefied natural gas is also imported from Algiers and some is produced domestically.

A new 300-kilometer-long pipeline named "Blue Stream" is being laid under the Black Sea to bring more natural gas from Russia. Two steel pipes, each one meter in diameter, are being laid at a depth of 2,100 meters. Pipelines have never before been laid so deep in the ocean. The Italian ENI is involved in realizing this daring project in partnership with the Russian Gazprom.

Critics claim that the "Blue Stream" will give Russia a monopoly as a supplier of natural gas. Critics also claim that the gas purchased by Turkey from Russia will have been originally purchased by Russia from Turkmenistan, and therefore Turkey would be better off purchasing gas directly from Turkmenistan. Negotiations have been going on between Turkey and Turkmenistan for the purchase of gas. Turkmenistan has refused to allocate some of its gas to a natural gas pipeline, which will be built parallel to the Baku-Tblisi-Ceyhan oil pipeline. This pipeline will bring natural gas to Turkey from the Shahdeniz field of Azerbaijan.

Purchase of gas from Azerbaijan is one of the several projects Turkey has undertaken in order to diversify its sources of natural gas. By the end of the summer of 2001, Turkey had purchased natural gas from Iran for a period of 25 years. The initial flow of three billion cubic meters per year will rise to ten billion cubic meters per year by 2005. In 2001, an agreement was also signed to purchase gas from Iraq. Most of the natural-gas purchasing agreements are based on the "take or pay" system (TOP), which obligates Turkey to pay for specified quantities even if the purchase is not needed. Critics claim that if all projects are realized and domestic demand does not grow as fast, Turkey may end up with an excess supply of natural gas and that excessive burdens will be imposed on the economy because of the nature of TOP agreements. During the second half of this decade, Turkey may find itself paying $700 million per year for gas that it does not need. Some or all of this burden may be alleviated through re-export to Europe.

Electric Production and Consumption: Per-capita electricity consumption is about 1,900 kWh and is expected to reach 4,000 kWh by the year 2010 and 6,000 kWh by 2020. Electric consumption increases by 8% annually. Demand is expected to reach 295 billion kWh in 2010 and double again in 2020. Industry consumes 54% of all electricity produced; houses consume 23%; businesses consume 8%; and government offices consume 5%. 8% is lost during distribution. 17% of total electricity production is stolen.

Country	Per capita Electricity Consumption (kWh)
USA	11,130
Germany	6,740
EU Average	4,925
Italy	3,665
Spain	3,270
Greece	2,862
Portugal	2,067
Turkey	1,900

PER CAPITA ELECTRICITY CONSUMPTION IN SELECTED COUNTRIES

The installed electricity production capacity was 27,000 MW as of August 2000, and annual production capacity was 160 billion kWh.

In 1999, total electricity produced remained at 116.5 billion kWh and total consumption at 119 billion kWh. The deficit was imported from Bulgaria, Georgia, and Iran.

60% of electricity is produced by the government-owned company TEAS, 15% by companies in which TEAS has a partnership, 10% by private companies, and 15% by industrialists who produce primarily for their own use.

Electric production increased by 4.6% annually during 1973–1993, the highest rate among OECD countries. (The OECD average for the same period was .8%.) 71.7% of electricity is obtained from thermal sources (33% from natural gas, up from 17.8% in 1990; 30% from lignite; 2.7% from coal; and 6% from fuel oil) and 27.5% from hydro sources. 0.1% of electricity is obtained from geothermal and 0.7% from other sources. The first station utilizing wind power was started at Cesme, near Izmir, in 1998. The plans to build a nuclear power plant at Akkuyu, on the Mediterranean, were shelved in 2001, mainly due to protests by conservationists who pointed out that the plant could meet no more than 3% of Turkey's energy needs yet would have very high economic and environmental costs.

It is estimated that in order to meet the rising energy demand, Turkey needs to annually create new energy capacity equivalent to that of Ataturk Dam (see next section). The country is currently utilizing only 30% of her hydro, 54% of her thermal, and 3% of her geothermal resources. By the year 2008, 36 more dams will have been constructed, bringing the level of utilization of hydro resources up to 43%. Also, by the year 2010, 33 new lignite, 12 new coal, and 14 new natural-gas power stations will have been built. Even if all these investments are realized, Turkey's per-capita energy production will have reached 3,250 kWh by 2010, which is about 60% of current European average and below the expected level of demand in Turkey (4000 kWh).

In its haste to meet energy needs the government has commissioned several new plants powered by natural gas. Among the several newly commissioned natural gas stations, the four under construction at Gebze, Adapazari, and Izmit will each be of 777 MW magnitude. Total production at these four plants will equal one quarter of all electricity currently produced in Turkey.

Critics point out that natural-gas-powered power plants are rare in Western Europe and that natural gas is a costly raw material for Turkey where total natural gas resources are equal to imports in a given year. Total oil resources are equal to oil imported in two years.

Several of the new natural-gas power stations were commissioned with a state guarantee to purchase all of their output. This is the "TOP" or "take or pay" system. The additional burden, which would be imposed on Turkish economy due to such arrangements during the course of the coming decade alone, was estimated to be equal to all external debt accumulated by the Turkish Republic since its founding eighty years ago. In 2001 the government effectively voided such contracts. The IMF and World Bank supported this move.

In addition to the 36 hydro power stations under construction, as of January 2002 there were 319 projects waiting to be implemented, with a total capacity of 7.8 MW. However, hydro power is proving to be more and more costly as rainfall declines, seemingly because of long-term climate change. Hydro power projects also raise serious environmental concerns.

Likely sources of cheap energy are wind, geothermal, and coal. The Marmara and Aegean regions and the southeast are promising in terms of wind power. Turkey's wind power potential is estimated as 83,000 MW. 1,700 MW of this power has been realized. 55 more wind power projects are waiting for approval.

Turkey is seventh in the world in terms of its geothermal resources. The cost of geothermal energy is one seventh the cost of natural gas, one sixth of oil and one fifth of coal. Geothermal energy potential of Turkey is estimated as 31,500 MW, which is equal to 30 billion cubic meters of natural gas. Currently, 52,000 residences are heated using geothermal energy. This figure could be raised to 5 million, if all geothermal energy potential were utilized.

Turkey will be self sufficient in coal for the next hundred years. The share of coal in electricity production in the US is 56%, as compared with 32.7% in Turkey. New technology makes it possible to produce clean energy using coal. The cost of electricity produced at coal-powered plants is 2.0–3.5 cents per kWh as compared with recently commissioned natural gas stations where the cost is 4.0–4.7 cents per kWh.

Another way to increase power output in Turkey would be through raising efficiency in production and distribution. 8% of all electricity produced in Turkey is lost during distribution. At any given point in time, Turkey utilizes no more than 70% of her power production capacity. Production at coal plants is 10 billion kWh below capacity because the type of coal used is not appropriate. If full-capacity utilization of power stations were possible, total electricity production would be nearly half as much more.

Mineral Resources: Even though Turkey is rich in mineral resources, mining constituted no more than roughly 0.8% of Turkey's GNP in 1907–1913 and 2.5% during recent decades. During 1981–1995, average growth rate was roughly 5% for the economy as a whole and 3% for mining. The main reason is the lack of investment. Until 1994, the government undertook 80% of mining investment. This ratio is now reversed and private companies are undertaking 70% of mining investment. Mineral exploration has been largely undertaken by the Mineral Research and Exploration Institute (MTA) and Etibank, which are both government owned. Since the mid-1950s, oil and natural gas exploration has been undertaken largely by foreign companies and by the government-owned Turkish Petroleum Corporation. The discovery of very large oil and natural gas deposits is not expected.

Roughly 12 metallic and 40 industrial minerals were mined in Turkey in 1996. Borate deposits, which are estimated to be over 2 billion tons, are probably the largest known in the world. The main borate deposits are in Eskisehir, Kutahya, and Balikesir provinces. In accordance with legislation enacted in 1978, the government-owned Etibank owns all borate operations. Chromite deposits are important worldwide because of their high chrome/iron ratio. There are over 300 magnetite deposits throughout the country, with the main concentration in west and central Turkey.

Large parts of Turkey are covered by metamorphosed limestone that has been transformed into marble of different colors and textures. Large deposits are in Afyon, Ankara, Balikesir, Bursa, Bilecik, Denizli, Mugla, Eskisehir, Izmir, and Kutahya. Proven trona reserves are 196 million tons, whereas probable trona reserves are 37 million tons. A trona deposit was found in 1979 in Beypazari County of Ankara. The Lake Van region in eastern Turkey is a potential source of trona. Trona reserves of the Lake Van itself, which has 22 grams salt per liter in its water, are about five billion tons. Moderate-value industrial mineral deposits such as dolomite, rock salt, cement raw materials, glass and ceramics minerals, refractory clays, and zeolites are very large in size. Other reasonably large deposits are copper, lead-zinc in metals, alumina minerals, bentonites, perlite, pumice, celestite, sodium sulphate, and trona in industrial minerals.

Total workable reserves of coal deposits along the western Black Sea Coast, which have been mined since 1865, are 700 million tons. The coal seams extend from 400 meters above sea level to 1300 meters below sea level. The remaining reserves, which are mostly under sea level, are generally highly inclined and extend under the Black Sea. Lignite deposits are widespread throughout Turkey. Heat values vary from 1100 to 4500 Kcal/kg per kg and sulfur content is generally high.

The lignite at the largest deposit of Afsin-Elbistan, which has roughly 3.4 million tons reserves, has a low heat value of 1050 Kcal/kg and 2.0 percent sulfur content.

Workable reserves with gold content are 76.6 tons. Potential gold reserves are 17 tons, and reserves of heavy metals associated with gold are 42 tons. In 1992, 8 foreign companies had 493 mining permits to explore gold in Turkey. A Turkish subsidiary of Gencor of South Africa owns deposits west of Ankara and southeast of Edremit. Normandy of Australia has started to produce gold at Turkey's largest gold deposit at Ovacik, Bergama. Residents of Ovacik, which is an extremely fertile agricultural region, are strongly opposed to the operation, which employs cyanide in refining gold, and are engaged in a much-publicized legal battle to halt the production. The concerns of locals are heightened by the fact that the area is located on faults and potentially prone to earthquakes.

Minerals that are imported in large volumes are metallurgical coal, iron ore, phosphate rock, sulfur and its products, and gold. Like her Middle East neighbors, Turkey is a large importer of gold bullion. It is estimated that during the past six decades, more than 2500 tons of gold bullion were imported into Turkey. Until 1985, gold imports were not legal and took place through illegal channels. Following the lifting of the ban on imports of gold bullion in 1985, there has been an outflow of $9 billion for gold. The total value of crude oil imports during the same period was roughly $20 billion. Supporters of gold production in Turkey claim that the protests of conservationists are organized by gold traders abroad who fear losing their markets in Turkey.

The main exports of minerals and mineral products are borate minerals and boron chemicals, chromite and ferrochrome, all types of magnetite, dimension stone, ceramics raw materials, barite, celestite, clinker and cement, ceramics, glass products, and steel products for which iron ore, scrap, and blum are imported in large quantities.

All mineral resources are under the jurisdiction of the State. Entrepreneurs can engage in mining with a government permit. The area of land where one can explore is unlimited, with the exceptions of marble, which is limited to 250 hectares, and of lake minerals, which are limited to 2000 hectares. The operation license, which can be extended to sixty years, is preceded by exploration and pre-operation licenses. In addition to payments of annual levies, which vary according to the nature of license, cash deposits, which are doubled every five years, are required to discourage the holding of large areas of land and as collateral for possible fines that may be imposed for failure to perform the actions required by law. (Source: Fuat I. Karayazici, *Mining in Turkey: An Economic Appraisal.*)

AGRICULTURE

Main Agricultural Products: Turkey is the world's largest producer of hazelnuts, apricots, figs, dried raisins, and eggplant, and the world's second largest producer of pistachios, chickpeas, lentils, and peppers.

Turkey produces 75% of the world's hazelnuts. Spain, Italy, and the USA produce the rest, with Spain being the second-largest producer. Exporters aim at keeping hazelnut prices low in order to discourage other countries from entering the market.

35% of the world's figs (70–75% of world fig exports) and 20% of the world's apricots are produced in Turkey. There are 10 million apricot and 9 million fig trees in the country.

Turkey is the second-largest producer of pistachios after Iran. 30% of world pistachio production is realized in Turkey.

In terms of vineyards, Turkey, with 800,000 hectares, is the fifth-largest country after Spain (1.7 hectares), Italy (1.4 hectares), the USSR (1.3 hectares), and France (1.2 hectares). 60% of all vineyards in Asia are in Turkey. Turkey is the sixth-largest grape producer after Italy, France, the former USSR, Spain, and the USA. 35% of world dried-raisin production takes place in Turkey.

MAIN PRODUCTS BY REGIONS	
Area	Main Agricultural Products
Black Sea	Tobacco, hazelnuts, maize
Central Turkey	Wheat, barley, oats, lentils, chickpeas (About a quarter of all wheat produced in Turkey is from Central Anatolia.)
Mediterranean	Citrus, cotton, rice
Aegean	Olives, figs, cotton, tobacco, grapes, raisins, apples, wheat
Marmara	Sunflowers, rice, wheat, olives, grapes. (64 % of all sunflower seeds produced in Turkey is from the Marmara region.)
Eastern Turkey	Husbandry

Turkey is the world's fourth-largest producer of olives after Spain, Italy, and Greece. Domestic consumption is around 160 thousand tons. It is estimated that there are 90 million olive trees in the country, compared with 185 million in Spain, 160 million in Italy, 120 million in Greece, and 60 million in Tunisia. Total production of olives is 120 thousand tons (900 thousand tons in Spain, 400 thousand tons in Italy, 350 thousand tons in Greece, and 185 thousand tons in Tunisia). Per-capita olive oil consumption is only 1 liter, compared with 26 liters in Greece, 17 liters in Italy, and 14 liters in Spain.

The production of citrus fruits meets Turkey's domestic demands, and some is exported. Turkey's share of the world output is about 3%, and Turkey is the eleventh-largest producer in the world.

Turkey is the sixth-largest producer of tobacco after the USA, China, India, Brazil, and the USSR, and the world's sixth-largest producer of cotton after China, the USA, India, Pakistan, and Uzbekhistan.

Area Cultivated: Turkey is one of 19 countries that has no further land reserves. Since 1960, arable land per capita has decreased from 9.5 decars to 4 decars, which is the ratio in developed countries. The total arable land is 235 thousand sq. km (30% of total). Only 6.5% of arable land is first quality; 9% second quality; and 10% is third quality. About one quarter of arable land lies fallow every year. Fertilizers are used on 60% of the arable land. 55% of the arable land can be irrigated and half of this total is. Two-thirds of the arable land is harvested for seed crops. 1.4% of the land is under protection as national park land. This ratio is 10.8% in developed counties.

Sizes of Land Holdings: Land holdings vary from 2 or 3 hectares up to 3,000. The advantages of large holdings become obvious as machine planting and harvesting spreads. However, holdings tend to be split up due to inheritance laws. Fragmentation of land holdings reduces yield and efficiency.

Yield in Agriculture: Overall yield is low in agriculture. Even though agricultural products make up only 16% of the GNP, 51% of the total labor force is employed in agriculture (9% in the EU). The number of those employed in agriculture in Turkey is equal to the total number of those employed in agriculture in the EU countries.

The yield per hectare is high in certain agricultural products. For example, yield in potato output is 22.7 tons per hectare. This figure is 24 tons in Austria and 34 tons in France. The yield per hectare is 3,113 kilos in rice, 817 kilos in cotton, 1,630 kilos in sunflowers, and 924 kilos in tobacco. The yield per hectare in wheat is 2.1 tons in Turkey, 8 tons in Holland, 7 tons in the UK, 6.8 tons in France, 6.3 tons in Germany,

5.4 tons in New Zealand, 5 tons in the USA, 4.8 tons in Italy, 3.6 tons in Greece, 2.7 tons in Canada, 2.2 tons in Israel, and 2 tons in Australia. Yields are higher on the milder coastal regions as compared with the colder and drier central and eastern regions. For example, in the Marmara region, yield per hectare in wheat is 50% higher than the national average. Except for a few varieties of corn and sunflowers, seeds are almost exclusively imported from abroad. Annually, 7,000 tons of seeds are imported mainly from Holland, Israel, and the USA. Yield of milk per cow is 1,700kg. The same figure is 4,081 kg in Greece.

Agricultural Mechanization: There are 57 tractors per 1000 persons employed in agriculture. This ratio is 3 in less developed countries and 877 in developed countries.

Growth of Agricultural Production: The growth of output in agriculture has been lagging behind the growth rate of the population. Since 1976, the population has increased by 47%, but agricultural output has increased by only 30%. The increase in population during the past decade is 19% and the increase in agricultural production 16%. According to FAO statistics, the per-capita agricultural output has decreased by about 7% since 1980. During the same period, animal stock fell by 15%.

Self-sufficiency in Food Production: In the not-too-distant past, Turkey claimed self-sufficiency in food production. This was probably an illusion because food production never exceeded the minimum food requirements of the population. During recent years, there has been an increase in food imports. The total volume of food imports in 1996 was $5 billion, half of which was spent on meat. Wheat, sugar, sunflowers, cotton, and rice were other major imports. Imports of fresh vegetables and fruits remain low. The total volume of fresh vegetable and fruit imports was 63 million dollars in 1998 or 0.2% of total imports.

Husbandry: The total number of stock animals is 55 million. 24% of the total is cattle, 60% sheep, and 16% goats. 15% of goats are native Angora. Average yield of milk per cow is quite low at 1,700 kg (4,081 kg in Greece). During the previous decade there was a continuous decline in the number of stock animals, mainly due to PKK terrorism in the southeast. On the other hand, there has been a major increase in poultry. The number of poultry in Turkey has risen from 61 million in 1987 to 175 million in 1997. Turkey is a leading country in honey production. There are 350,000 horses and 640,000 donkeys in the country.

Fishing: The annual fish catch is 500,000 tons. 7% of all fish are caught in fresh water. The annual fish catch per person is about 9 kilos. The world average annual fish catch per person is 19 kilos, compared with 493 kilos in Norway, 332 kilos in Denmark, 103 kilos in Japan, and 20.5 kilos in the USA.

Forests: The forest area per capita is 0.35 hectares. 26% of Turkey is classified as forest, while 18.7% of Canada, 7.2% of Australia and 1.2% of the world as a whole is. Approximately 11 million hectares (half) of the forest area is now unproductive and the mature forested area is decreasing due to various factors such as land used for agriculture, uncontrolled razing, and forest fires. The Forestry Department has a large-scale reforestation program. The success of this program depends on the improvement of the social and economic conditions of forest villagers. Measures are being taken towards this end.

Turkey's forests have great variation, ranging from cone-bearing, needle-leaf evergreen forest to forests with deciduous trees belonging to the mild climate zones. However, present forest-management strategies are timber-production oriented and do not incorporate the value of forests from a more comprehensive perspective as genetic-resource reservoirs.

Erosion: Rapid land erosion is taking place because of wrong land use, overgrazing, and deforestation. Erosion is proceeding 17 times faster than the rate in Europe and 6 times faster than the rate in North America. Annually, 500 million tons of topsoil is lost due to erosion. If erosion continues at its present rate, 85% of the country will have turned into desert by 2010. During the past decade, Turkey's meat imports increased by 2000%. Ecologists claim erosion is the reason. During the same period, Turkey lost 40% of its top soil and half of its pasture land.

Support for Agriculture: In the 1970s, the government supported 25 agricultural products. As of 1999 only the production of grains, sugar beets, and tobacco were receiving government support. In 1999, government support per person employed in agriculture was $344, compared with $1,400 in Portugal, $4,000 in Greece, $6,300 in Germany, $9,700 in France, and $15,800 in Ireland. The EU average was $6,133 (Yakup Kepenek, *Cumhuriyet*, March 29, 1999). According to the figures provided by OECD in 1997, agricultural supports were 7% of the GNP of OECD countries. Turkish consumers paid 85% of agricultural supports. The same ratio was 60% for OECD countries as a whole.

Despite agricultural supports, terms of trade have deteriorated for farmers. One kilo of bread, which was worth two kilos of wheat in 1980, was worth five kilos in 1988 (*Cumhuriyet*, October 16, 1999). In 1999, wholesale prices rose by 62.9% and consumer prices rose by 68.8%, compared with the 41.6% rise in agricultural prices. This means that in 1999 the relative price of farm products dropped by 27.2% and the incomes of farmers fell roughly by $10 billion (Gungor Uras, *Milliyet* 4/2/2000).

As of 2002, support for all agricultural products was lifted and most of the institutions and organizations set up to support agriculture was either privatized or abolished. Annually, farmers were supposed to receive "direct income support," which would not be more than $400 per year per farmer. (Average "direct income support" for each American farm is $30,000.) However, insufficient budget allocations meant that farmers would not even receive as much.

SOUTHEAST ANATOLIA PROJECT

The Project: The Southeast Anatolia Project (Guneydogu Anadolu Projesi or GAP) consists of 22 dams (8 on the Tigris, 14 on the Euphrates) and 19 hydraulic power stations that are being constructed on the Euphrates and Tigris rivers, two 26.4 km-long irrigation tunnels, and the related 4000 km-long network of irrigation channels. Estimated cost of the project is 32 billion dollars, 12.6 billion dollars of which has already been spent. 57% of energy production has been completed. 60% of the total amount spent has been retrieved by electric production at Ataturk and Karakaya dams.

The project will affect an area of 73,863 square km. This area would equal 9.2% of the area of Turkey, or 239% of Belgium, 176% of Holland, or 74% of South Korea. Currently, approximately 8% of Turkey's population lives in the GAP area. By the year 2012, 16% of Turkey's population will be living in the same area because of internal migration triggered by new employment opportunities. After the completion of the project, 1,633,000 hectares of land will be irrigated. This is equal to 8% of all agricultural land in Turkey and to 20% of all arable land. When the project is complete, the annual food production of Turkey will have risen sufficiently to feed an additional population of 80 million persons, and additional jobs will have been created for 3.8 million persons.

It is expected that agricultural yield will increase 17 times after irrigation. This means that the project will lead to a doubling of Turkey's agricultural output. Farms will be able to plant three crops annually and grow cotton, corn, soybeans, fruit, vegetables, and flowers. It is expected that the value of agricultural production in the region, which was $800 million in 1980, will be boosted to $6.6 billion by 2010. Total electricity produced by the dams in the project is 27.3 billion kilowatt hours. This is equal to one quarter of Turkey's present annual electricity production.

The implementation of the project has already had a major impact on the economy of southeast Turkey. The economic growth rate for Turkey as a whole was 4.7% between 1983 and 1996 but 7% in southeast Turkey.

Ataturk Dam: The most important part of the Southeast Anatolia Project is the Ataturk Dam, which was constructed on the Euphrates near Urfa. The 169-meters-high dam, which can hold 49 billion cubic meters of water, is the fourth largest in the world. Water will be transmitted from the dam to the Harran plains in Urfa through two tunnels that are 26.4 km long each. The Ataturk Dam will irrigate 1.4 million hectares of land, which is approximately equal to 6% of all arable agricultural land in Turkey. The dam will produce 9 billion kilowatt hours of electricity, which is equal to approximately 10% of current electric production.

The construction site of the dam was the largest in the world. 7,262 persons, including 210 engineers and 1,300 drivers, were employed daily in the construction. Concrete used in construction would have been sufficient to build 55,000 residences, each covering an area of 100 sq. meters. A Turkish company constructed the Ataturk dam. A Swiss company supplied turbines and generators. Daily expenditures during construction were $750,000 and the total cost was $2.5 billion. Financing was realized exclusively by the Turkish government because international institutions refused to participate due to the opposition from Turkey's neighbors. The dam paid for itself in one year through sales of electricity.

Ecological Problems: Implementation of the project is leading to ecological problems. Humidity in the affected area has risen from 30% to 90%, leading to a proliferation of insects. Farmers, who needed to spray pesticides only 4 times annually now spray 10–15 times. Because of insufficient drainage, 3 tons of salt accumulate per hectare following each irrigation period.

TRADE, FOREIGN INVESTMENT, TOURISM

Imports and Exports: Despite the overall decline in world trade during 1990–1996, Turkey's trade continued to increase annually at the rate of 11% compared to 4.5% for the EU, 7.5% for North America, and 7% for Japan. Imports rose by 154% and exports rose by 124% during the 1990s. In 1999, because of the recession the country experienced, exports dropped by 18% and imports dropped by 6%, compared with the previous year. The effort to keep the exchange rate stable, part of the fight against inflation, led to a major deterioration in the trade balance in 2000. In 2000, imports rose by 32.7% and exports rose only by 2.8%. In 2000, exports, which are usually roughly 65% of imports, dropped to 50.6%.

64

Following the devaluations that took place at the end of 2000 and in February 2001, export revenues rose by 12.5% and imports dropped by 26% in 2001, as compared with 2000, when measured in US dollars. The rise in exports was 17.7% and the drop in imports was 19.2% during the same period, when measured in Euros. Consequently, the trade deficit dropped by 65%, from $26 billion in 2000 to $9.3 billion in 2001. The trade deficit is financed through tourism revenues (roughly 30% of the deficit), remittances sent home by workers abroad (roughly 20% of the deficit), and the "suitcase trade" (50% of the deficit in 1997). Roughly 90% of Turkey's foreign exchange revenues are needed to meet export expenditures.

COMPOSITION OF IMPORTS AND EXPORTS (2001)			
Main Export Items	(%)	Main Import Items	(%)
Industrial Products	92	Industrial Products	80.5
Agricultural Products	7	Agricultural Products	3.5
Minerals	1	Minerals	16

The manufacturing base of the country was built through import substitution. Yet import substitution failed to encourage the evolution of competitive industries. According to the Swiss Management Development Institute, Turkey is the 34th with 34.5 points, amongst 39 nations in terms of the competitiveness of its economy (*Hürriyet*, April 25, 2001). The USA is the first with100 points; Canada is 9th with 76.9 points; Australia is 11th with 75.9 points; Germany is 12th with 74 points, Israel is 13th with 67.9 points, the UK is 16th with 64.8 points, New Zealand is 17th with 61.7 points; Greece is 20th with 49.9 points; Brazil is 21st with 49.7 points; Italy is 22nd with 49.6 points; China is 23rd with 49.5 points; South Africa is 32nd with 38.6 points; and Russia is 35th with 35.4 points.

Turkey has shifted its comparative advantage in international trade from agriculture to industry and services. Since 1980, the share of agriculture in Turkey's total exports has dropped from 57% to 7% and the share of industry and services

MAIN TRADING PARTNERS OF TURKEY (2001)			
Country	(%) Share of Turkey's Exports	Country	(%) Share of Turkey's Imports
Germany	17	Germany	13
USA	10	Italy	8.4
Italy	7.5	Russia	8.3
UK	7	US	7.9
France	6	Switzerland	1.7

has increased from 36% to 92%. Manufacturing strength is in textiles, automotive, steel, chemicals, cement, consumer durable goods, and glass industries. Textiles have been by far the fastest growing export industry. Textiles make up 40% of all exports. Other industries such as steel and electronics have begun to gain ground.

Trade Issues: Turkey is an associate member of the EU and has entered into full customs union with the union in January 1996. Turkey had started the painful but necessary process of reducing tariffs in such key industries as textiles, automobiles, consumer durable goods, and cement as early as 1993. All tariffs on industrial products and processed food were greatly reduced in 1996. As of 1998, the average protection rate against the EU was only 5.29%.

As a result of customs union, legislation concerning competition and intellectual property rights was strengthened in Turkey. Turkish consumers benefit from reduced prices for a variety of products and European consumers benefit from the elimination of quotas on Turkish textiles and garments.

Following the implementation of the customs union, Turkey had a drop in tariff revenues by $2.6 billions. This loss was to be compensated by $3.5 billion support, which was to be paid to Turkey by the EU over a period of five years. However, this support was not realized for many years because of a Greek veto.

The share of EU countries in Turkey's imports has risen from 47% to 53% and the share of EU countries in Turkey's exports has declined from 51% to 49%. Turkey has become the EU's largest supplier of textile products. 70% of Turkish-produced clothing and 40% of textile exports go to the EU. Turkish suppliers meet 11.5% of EU demand for textiles. Yet, because of the general drop in demand in Europe, hoped-for increases in textiles, glass, leather, processed food, ceramics, and steel exports were not realized.

Customs union with the EU prevents Turkey from developing special economic relationships with third parties. The EU, on the other hand, imposed an anti-dumping tax against Turkey without prior consultation and has introduced new restrictions with regard to the trade of agricultural goods. Turkey is being pressured to cut sugar beet production from 15 million tons to 6 million tons. EU countries export the sugar they produce at one third of cost. EU has taken anti-dumping action against Turkish steel and started an anti-dumping investigation against Turkish TV sets.

Turkey faces anti-dumping action by a number of other countries. Canada, Argentina, Singapore, and the USA have taken action against various types of Turkish steel. The USA has taken anti-dumping action against Turkish spaghetti and aspirin, and Israel against fresh fruit.

Following the Gulf War, Turkey was obligated to comply with the embargo against Iraq, whereas countries like Jordan were given exemptions and were allowed to continue their trade with Iraq. In 1989 alone, Turkey's exports to Iraq were worth $1.7 billion. This figure was equal to 15% of Turkey exports during that year. Exports to Gulf countries, which were transported through Iraq, amounted to another $1.3 billion. Turkey's total loss in exports to Iraq and to the Gulf countries during the decade since the Gulf war is therefore estimated as $30 billion. This is assuming, of course, that exports would have remained stable and not increased as would actually be expected during the course of the decade. The closing of the oil pipeline from Iraq has cost Turkey another $40 billion since the Gulf war.

Loss of trade with Iraq and the Gulf has been particularly damaging for the southeastern region of Turkey. The only competitive advantage this region possesses is its proximity to Iraq and to the Gulf countries via Iraq. Before the war, 150 thousand vehicles were employed in the trade with Iraq and other Gulf countries. These trucks and the 2000 service stations along their routes were the source of livelihood of an estimated 4 million people.

Even though Turkey is in customs union with the EU, Turkey's exports to the USA are subject to quota and tariff restrictions, whereas the exports of EU member countries are not. The tax on Turkish exports to the USA is 15–35% whereas the Turkish taxes on imports from the USA is 8%. On the other hand, the US government claims that Turkey imposes non-tariff barriers against imports from the USA. The US government is particularly unhappy about the non-tariff barriers such as "import" and "health" certificates, which apply to health and food products.

60% of Turkey's exports to the US are realized by the textile industry. Lifting of the US quotas on textile imports from Turkey would lead to an additional volume of exports of $3 billion. It is hard to understand why the US is not being more conciliatory with Turkish demands, as the annual volume of Turkey's exports is so insignificant in the total volume of US imports. The annual volume of US imports is $1.2 trillion; the total volume of annual Turkish exports to the US is 3 billion, or only 0.25% of the total.

Ultimately, Turkey would like the lifting of quotas and tariffs in trade with the US. Turkey would also like to start qualified industrial zones (QIZ) like those the US has in Jordan and Israel. Production realized in those zones can be exported as US products, which would help to overcome the US quotas against Turkey.

"Suitcase Trade": Following the collapse of the socialist regimes in Eastern Europe and Russia, a new form of trade emerged between the freshly emerging capitalists from these countries and Turkey: the so-called "suitcase trade." Tourists from those countries arriving in Turkish towns (mainly Istanbul, but also the Black Sea port Trabzon and some others) and fill their "suitcases" with merchandise that they sell at home. This form of trade is a relatively inexpensive way of supplying the consumers from these countries with much-needed consumer goods and is a very important source of international currency for Turkey. The annual volume of sales to suitcase traders was $10 billion in 1997, which was equal to half of Turkey's official trade deficit. In 1997 on the average, 25 busses, 5 cruise ships and 3 planes daily brought Eastern European and Russian tourists engaged in the suitcase trade to Turkey. In Istanbul, there were 40,000 shops specializing in the suitcase trade employing 200,000 workers. 12,000 Turkish manufacturers were producing mainly for suitcase traders. The main items demanded by suitcase traders were textiles, leather, biscuits, detergents, soap, vegetables, and fruit. The suitcase trade was affected negatively by the economic developments in Russia and was cut in half in 1998 and by 60% in 1999. The suitcase trade was equal to 10% of total exports in 1999. The suitcase trade rose again during subsequent years. The increase during the first half of 2001 was 43.5% over 2000.

Foreign Investment: Turkey is one of the 15 largest and also one of the fastest growing markets of the world and should therefore be attractive for international investors. Favorable relations with neighboring markets, favorable regulations, well-developed infrastructure, and rich human resources are other factors that contribute to the attraction of Turkey for international capital.

Nevertheless, foreign investment remains low. Turkey's share of worldwide international investment is 0.015%, compared with 31% for the USA, 11% for the UK, and 7% for China. The total volume of foreign investment in Turkey is 9% of the GNP, compared with 60% in Malaysia, 40% in Chile, 18% in Greece, 17% in Brazil, 14% in Argentina and Mexico, and 6% in South Korea. As of 2001, per-capita foreign investment in Turkey is $15, compared with $4080 in Ireland and $85 in China.

In 1999, 0.09% of foreign investment in the world took place in Turkey. The volume of annual foreign investment was nearly doubled following the legislation of a law in 1999 that introduced arbitration by international referees with regard to disputes concerning foreign investment. The total volume of foreign investment realized in Turkey up to the year 2001 was $14.207 billion. This figure is far from being impressive as foreign investment realized in the year 2001 only was

$105 billion in China. During the same year, $10 billion was invested in Poland, $3.5 billion in Malaysia, $2.1 billion in Vietnam and in Slovakia, and $982 million in Turkey. In 2001, Turkey was 121st out of 136 nations in terms of the volume of foreign investment realized.

One of the reasons why Turkey fails to attract foreign investment is bureaucracy. It is estimated that 20% of management activities in Turkey are taken over by bureaucratic procedures. On the average, granting of an investment permit requires 172 signatures and two and a half months. The permission for an energy project that took fourteen months to build took nine years to be approved. In terms of the bureaucracy necessary in order to start a new company, Turkey is the worst in Europe, followed by Italy, France, and Spain. According to the World Economic Forum, in terms of negative impact of bureaucracy on the economy, Turkey is the tenth among fifty-nine nations (*Isveren*, Monthly Publication of Turkish Employers' Union, November 2002).

14% of foreign investment is in automotive, 14% in banking, 10% in commerce, 7% in electronics, 6.5% in tobacco, 6% in food, 6% in chemicals, and 6% in tourism. 60% of foreign investment is by EU firms (19% Holland, 18% France, 11% Germany, 5% Italy, 5% England, 11% USA, and 8% Japan.) Foreign firms have partnerships in 5,470 Turkish companies. 27% of partnerships are with German firms, 11% with Dutch, 11% with British, 10% with Iranian, 9% with French, 7% with Italian, 6% with Swiss, 6% with Iraqi, 5% with Russian, 4% with Austrian, 2% with Belgian, 2% with Japanese, and 2% with Greek. The number of partnerships with international firms and volume of foreign investment is expected to rise as Turkish companies increasingly seek international partnerships following the economic crisis in 2001.

Tourism: Turkey is rich in terms of tourist resources. The country has sunshine, one of the longest and cleanest shorelines along the Mediterranean (with 99 beaches and 11 marinas proudly hoisting the mark of cleanliness, the "Blue Banner"), 33,400 archaeological sites, 44,000 buildings of historical interest, and more than 100 ongoing archaeological excavations. In recent years there has been a marked improvement in tourism infrastructure. The total number of beds available for tourists has risen from 10,000 in 1963 to 550,000 in 1998. There are 4,200 travel agents and 7,000 tour guides. It is therefore not surprising that tourism has experienced a phenomenal growth during this time.

During 1983–1998, tourism revenues doubled every three years, rising from $411 million in 1983 to $8.3 billion in 1998. Total contribution to the GNP by tourism was $52 billion (25% of the current GNP) during 1983–1998. Tourism revenues were $7.6 billion in 2000. This amount equals 4% of the GNP (compared with 6% in Portugal, 3.9% in Greece, and 3.8% in Spain), 28% of exports, and 29% of the trade deficit during that year. It is estimated that tourism supports 32 auxiliary industries. Together with auxiliary industries, the share of tourism in the Turkish GNP is estimated as 17%.

A total of 1,250,000 people are employed in tourism. According to the World Tourism and Travel Council (WTTC) the contribution of tourism to the Turkish economy will continue to rise by 5.8% annually during the next decade, creating 1,500,000 new jobs. Total tourism revenues will have risen to $73.4 billion by 2010 (*Hürriyet*, May 1, 2000). The average investment needed to create one job in other sectors of the Turkish economy is $54,000, as compared with $43,000 in tourism.

During the past two decades, Turkey has had the highest growth rate among OECD countries in terms of number of tourists per capita. Yet this ratio remains relatively low, indicating great potential. The number of tourists coming to Turkey rose from 1,625,000 in 1983 to 9,700,000 in 1998 but dropped to 6.8 million in 1999, compared with France 71.4 million, Spain 52 million, the USA 47 million, Italy 36 million, China 27 million, the UK 25 million, and Greece 11.5 million. The total number of tourists visiting Turkey reached 12 million in 2001. In 1999, Turkey was the 21st-most-visited country in the world while France, followed by Spain, the USA, Italy, China, and the UK were the most visited.

Tourism revenues are not rising as fast. The main reason for this is the drop in per-capita expenditures per tourist. Per-capita expenditures by tourists have dropped from $735 in 1998 to $557 in 2001 (Gungor Uras, *Milliyet* July 21, 2001). The main cause for this drop is the marketing of "everything included" packages by tour operators. Tourists who buy such packages tend to remain locked up in "holiday villages" during the duration of their stay. In Greece, a shifting of emphasis from "package tours" resulted in a rise of per-capita tourist expenditures from $559 in 1998 to $744 in 2000. The buying power exerted by tour

TOURISTS PER CAPITA AND PER SQ. KM IN OECD COUNTRIES				
Country	Tourists/ Capita in 1972	Tourists/ Capita in 1992	Tourists/ sq. km in 1972	Tourists/ sq. km in 1992
Turkey	2.8	12.5	1.3	9.0
France	19.1	104.5	18.0	108.0
Greece	27.4	90.6	18.0	71.0
Italy	64.3	86.7	116.0	166.0
Portugal	45.5	89.7	43.0	97.0
Spain	94.4	141.9	64.0	110.0

operators who market package tours also contribute to a drop in tourism revenues. Three major tour operators market most of the hotels on Turkey's southern shore. This is probably the reason why hotel prices in Turkey are 30–40% cheaper than the prices in Turkey's competitors. Tour operators retain 60% of the fees they collect from their clients, leaving only 40% for the Turkish travel industry.

In 2001, 25% of tourists came from Germany, 7% from the UK, 5% from France, 5% from Holland, 4% from the USA, 3% from Italy, and 1% from Japan.

PUBLIC FINANCE

Budget Expenditures: In 2001, the volume of budget expenditures was equal to 43% of the GNP. The budget deficit was 37.5 % (30% in 2000) of total budget expenditures and 19% (10.5% in 2000) of the GNP. 50% of the budget was spent on debt service. Debt service was equal to 130% of total public revenues and 103% of total tax revenues (28% in 1992, 51% in 1994, and 77% in 2000). In 2001, 21% of the budget was spent on wages and salaries of government employees, 10.5% on defense and 5% on infrastructure investment. In terms of the share in the budget of social services such as education, health, and unemployment, Turkey is similar to countries such as Madagascar, Eritrea, and Yemen. In 2001, 8% of budget was spent on social security, 8% on education, and 2% on health. During 2002, public expenditures were expected to drop by 15% (debt service would drop by 7% and other expenditures would drop by 8%).

Tax Revenues: In 2002, the ratio of total tax revenues to the GNP was 20.6% (10% in 1968). This ratio was one of the lowest amongst OECD countries. Considering that nearly half of economic activities are not recorded, the ratio of total tax revenues to the GNP may be as low as 12%.

TAXATION RATES IN OECD COUNTRIES			
Country	Rate (%)	Country	Rate (%)
Denmark	56.0	New Zealand	36.0
Sweden	55.5	Canada	33.6
France	44.3	Switzerland	32.2
European Average	40.6	Australia	31.0
Greece	40.0	Japan	30.0
OECD Average	37.7	USA	30.0
Great Britain	37.7	Turkey	25.4
Germany	37.4	South Korea	23.0
Italy	37.1	Mexico	17.0

The main sources of direct tax revenue are the income tax and the value-added tax. The value-added tax makes up 33% of total tax revenues (18% in Europe), income tax 26%, tax on petroleum consumption 17% (75% of value price of gasoline is tax), and corporate tax 13%.

The value-added tax varies between 8–40%, but it is as low as 1% on essential items and 8% on books. For most goods, the value-added tax is 17% of the sale price of the goods.

The lowest income-tax bracket is 15% (compared with 10% in the UK, 11% in the USA, 15% in Japan, and 22% in Germany) and rises up to 40%. The wage-and-salary-earner share of the national income is about 25%. However, wage-and-salary earners pay about 51% of income tax. According to a study conducted by the Turkish Employers' Confederation in 2001, the tax burden on the average salary, including social security payments, was 48% during that year (34% in Greece, 33% in Spain, 30% in the USA, and 29% in Japan).

It is estimated that up to 68% of income is not declared in order to evade taxation (Dr. Turkmen Derdiyok, "Estimate of Turkey's Unofficial Economy," *Milliyet* June 6, 1993). Income taxes paid by profit, rent, and interest earners, who receive 75% of the GNP, make up 1.5% of the GNP (7–8% of the GNP in the USA and the UK). The corporate tax rate is 33%. In 2001, corporate tax revenues made up only 1.43% of total tax revenues; 85% of corporate tax was paid by 1448 companies.

A major tax reform was enacted in 1998 in order to remedy some of these problems and to increase the overall taxation rate. This reform reduced income tax rates but rendered all income taxable and brought taxpayers the obligation to explain the source of their expenditures. Interestingly, the recession, which followed the rise in taxes, led to a drop in tax revenues. During 2001, prices rose by 61.6% and tax revenues rose by 55%. This means a 4.2% drop in real tax revenues in 2001.

Wasteful Spending: It is a generally held view that public debt is partly due to wasteful spending. The total volume of domestic debt service ($106.8 billion) during 1996–2001 equals the total losses incurred in public contracts during 1986–2001 (TUSIAD, quoted by Oya Berberoglu, *Hürriyet,* February 25, 2001). As of 2001, there were 35 ministries in Turkey as compared with 15 in Germany, 14 in the USA and in France, and 12 in Japan. 335,000 residences and 162,000 telephone are provided free of charge for government employees. (Guneri Civaoglu, *Milliyet* October 17, 2000) The government owns 23,100 vehicles (9,000 in France, 10,000 in Japan, 12,000 in the UK, and 15,000 in Germany). During the first half of 2000 alone, $200 million was spent on the purchase of new vehicles for the government (Okay Gonensin, *Sabah*). 19 government-owned planes serve top level bureaucrats and politicians

(17 in Canada, 14 in Germany, 7 in Pakistan, 4 in Portugal, 3 in Norway, and 1 in Greece).

National Debt: Turkey is the eighth-most-indebted nation in the world. As of June, 2002, the domestic debt was $70 billion, or 58% of the GNP. External debt is $118 billion or 62% of the GNP, 350% of exports. Total national debt per person was nearly $3000. The total public debt as a share of GNP is roughly 136%. In Argentina, where a severe economic and social crisis was experienced in 2001, the ratio of external debt to GNP was only 45%. According to IMF and World Bank criteria, nations with public debt exceeding 50% of their GNP are considered to be heavily in debt. The EU demands the public debt for its member countries be below 60% of their GNP. Turkey aims at reducing public debt below 60% of the GNP by 2006.

The ratio of debt service to budget was 44% in 2000. The ratio of annual debt service to the GNP, which had been around 15% of the GNP during the previous years, rose to 22.5% in 2001. Total volume of debt service in 2001 was $30 billion. This amount is roughly equal to the $31.5 billion loan Turkey received from the IMF in 2002.

External debt service equals about 3% of the GNP and 40% of export earnings. 83% of external debt has accumulated during the past two decades. The breakdown of external debt servicing between interest and principle is around 2/3. 25% of external debt is short term. The volume of short-term external debt is as large as the export earnings. Approximately half of external debt is held by the public and the remaining half by the private sector.

One third of domestic debt is to private individuals and banks and the rest to banks owned by the government. Domestic debt rose by 77% during the first six months of 2001, following the assumption of the losses of public banks by the treasury. Public banks had incurred the losses on loans to the government.

LABOR

Employment: Roughly 23.7 million or 35% of the population are active in the labor force. 30% of all those who work are wage earners, the rest (70%) are self employed. 1.3% of the population are members of trade unions. 11% of the population receive transfer income from the government or from other sources. According to the State Institute of Statistics, the unemployment rate in 2001 was 8%. It was 11.6% in urban areas, 3.9% in rural areas; it was 8.5% for male and 6.9% for female workers. One-fifth of those who were unemployed lost their jobs in 2001. 5.7% of the labor force is under-employed. The unemployment rate for youth with post-secondary degrees is 28.7% (32.3% in cities) and the unemployment rate for the urban labor force is 17%. Half of those who are technically defined as unemployed have temporary jobs.

Wages and Productivity: According to the German journal *Focus*, in Germany, wage for similar labor is 2.26 times higher than in Turkey. The ratio is 1.45 for Greece, 1.97 for New Zealand, 2.24 for Australia, 2.39 for South Africa, 2.46 for the UK, 2.67 for the USA, and 2.68 for Japan. On the average, productivity is 2.81 times and wages are 4.51 times higher in Europe. (Source: MPM - National Productivity Center.)

Workers Abroad: There are approximately 1 million Turkish workers abroad. The number of Turks living abroad, including relatives of workers, is 3.5 million. The first Turkish workers to go abroad were those who went to the USA at the beginning of the twentieth century. A major migration took place to Western Europe, particularly to Germany, during the economic boom years of 1960s and the early 1970s. Following the oil crisis, labor migration changed its direction toward the Arab countries. Today, Turkish labor continues to migrate. However, the numbers of workers emigrating annually has dropped from 59,483 in 1995 to 16,516 in 1999 (Annual Central Bank report, 2000). New emigrants are employed mainly by Turkish construction companies, which have contracted work in the Arab countries and in the former Soviet Union. 60% of the workers who went abroad during the second half of the previous decade migrated to the former USSR and 15% to Saudi Arabia.

Turkish workers abroad make a major contribution to the Turkish economy through their remittances. Revenues from worker's remittance were $4.6 billion in 1999 or 17% of total exports, 17% of the trade deficit, and 2.3% of the GNP. Total remittances during the 1990–1999 period were $36 billion. Annually, Turkish workers in Germany send home to Turkey 2.5 billion DM in remittances. The annual savings of Turkish families in Germany are estimated as 30 billion DM, which is roughly equal to half of Turkey's annual budget.

Unemployment is widespread among workers who have previously immigrated to various European countries and to Central Asia. Half of Turkish workers in Central Asia are unemployed. Unemployment among Turkish workers is 26% in Germany, 30% in France, 40% in Holland, 16% in Austria, 39% in Belgium, 26% in Sweden, 7% in the UK, 35% in Denmark, and 18% in Switzerland. With the exception of the UK, where the overall unemployment rate is 5%, these rates are 2–5 times the overall unemployment rates in the respective countries. (*Sabah*, January 23, 2000.)

The demand for immigrant labor is expected to rise in Europe (*Sabah*, January 23, 2000). According to UN estimates, European countries will need 35 million more immigrant workers by 2025. In order to keep their population stable at 1995 levels, Italy will need to import 9 million and Germany will need to import 14 million workers by the year 2025. This means that between now and 2025, Germany will demand 500,000 workers annually and Italy will need 300,000. If Germany does not import labor, by 2050 the average age in Germany will have risen from 45 to 55 and the population will have dropped from 81 million to 40 million. Because of the acute need for imported labor, changes are taking place in several European countries in attitudes and policies toward immigrant labor. In many of these countries, immigrant labor and their families have been regarded as temporary and as guests. New policies are leaning toward treating them as permanent and therefore aiming toward assimilation. Germany recently enacted new immigration laws that make it easier for immigrants to acquire citizenship. Prior to that, German citizenship was reserved almost exclusively for those of German blood.

Turkish Workers in Germany: Turkish residents, who make up 2.3% of Germany's population, are by far the largest ethnic group in that country. More than two-thirds of the Turks in Germany have been living there for more than 10 years. More than half the Turks in Germany were born there. Annually 45,000 Turkish children are born in Germany and 70,000 Turks officially migrate to that country, while 40,000 return back to Turkey. 10% of Turks in Germany have German citizenship. Of the 2.4 million Turks who are over eighteen and living in Germany, 27% have chosen German citizenship. According to the new German citizenship law enacted in 1999 by the Social Democrat-Green Coalition, Turkish children born in Germany are granted dual citizenship and will have the opportunity to choose the citizenship of either country when they are 18. It is expected that the number of German citizens of Turkish origin reached 620,000 by the end of 2001 and will reach 900,000 by the end of 2003. The number of voters of Turkish origin who will be eligible to vote during the elections to be held in 2002, will be no less than 590,000. 70% of Turks who are German citizens vote for the Social Democrats and 17% vote for the Greens.

32% of Turks in Germany are in the 21–35 age group; 27% are younger than 15. The same ratio (younger than 15) is 16% for Germans. 500,000 Turkish students are studying in German schools. Of this number, 13,000 are in post-secondary education. The number of Turkish girls in higher education has increased 3 times since 1985. Presently, 32% of Turkish youth in German higher education are girls.

In 1998, only 14% of Turkish secondary-school graduates qualified for college, compared to more than 30% of their German counterparts. Language difficulties are behind the relative failure of Turkish students in Germany. Almost three quarters of Germany's Turkish residents live in urban ethnic enclaves with a network of shops, restaurants, mosques, and professional services. More than a dozen Turkish channels are available via cable or satellite. Those living in these enclaves do not need to know German to get along. According to one study, two-thirds of Turkish children in the Kreuzberg district of Berlin speak little or no German (*Time,* April 30, 2001, p. 29).

Salaries of Germans are on the average 17% higher than the salaries of Turkish employees doing similar work. Unemployment among Turks in Germany is 26%. 35% of all unemployed foreigners living in Germany are Turks.

Several former Turkish workers in Germany have become entrepreneurs. Turks own 18% of all economic enterprises in Germany. Turkish entrepreneurs in Germany own 51,000 businesses in 54 different industries with a total investment of 11.1 billion DM and total annual revenues of 46.1 billion DM. They pay 6 billion DM annually in taxes and employ 265,000 workers, 15% of which are Germans. 9.5% of Turkish-owned enterprises in Germany employ more than 10 workers. Originally concentrated in the retail and wholesale trade and in food businesses, Turkish businesses now include electronics, textiles, and tourism. Several Turkish-owned businesses in Germany are medium-to-large-scale. Turkish businesses in Germany are growing at the rate of 12% annually. It is expected that number of Turkish-owned businesses in Germany will reach 100,000 by 2010, employing one million workers and with total revenues of 200 billion DM.

Turkish savings in the German Central Bank alone are 9 billion DM. Annually, Turkish workers pay 80 billion DM in taxes to the German federal government (including 450 million DM for the development of East Germany) and 7 billion DM to the federal retirement fund. Annual payments to Turks out of the federal retirement fund are only 400 million DM. Turkish residents contribute to raise consumer demand in Germany. On the average, Turkish families in Germany have 4.1 members and German families have 2.35 members, which means that the consumption potential for the average Turkish family would be higher than the consumption potential for the average German family. Presently, Turkish families in Germany save 12% of their income. 15 years ago, this ratio was 45%. (All information in this section, except for the information on language problems of Turkish residents of Germany, which was taken from *Time,* was provided by the Turkish Research Center (TAM) located in Essen, Germany.)

Turkish Workers Abroad in Business: Many Turkish workers abroad have become entrepreneurs. According to the statistics provided by Turkish Labor Ministry and by the Turkish Studies Center (TAM) based in Essen, former Turkish workers abroad own roughly 80,000 enterprises. 2,700 Turkish-owned businesses are active in Australia. In Europe, Turkish worker-owned businesses specialize in construction, clothing, food, and services. In 1999 there were 73,200 Turkish-owned businesses in Europe, employing 366,000. 18,000 workers are employed by 7,500 Turkish-owned enterprises in Holland, which have a total revenue of 2,3 billion. There are 2,000 Turkish-owned businesses in Belgium, 3,500 in France, 1,500 in Denmark, 250 in Austria, 800 in Switzerland, and 1,000 in Sweden.

Turkish workers go to Middle Eastern countries specifically with the purpose of starting businesses. Because of the legal obstacles, Turks in those countries need to cooperate and form partnerships with locals. There are 2,100 Turkish-operated hairdresser shops, 3,2000 restaurants, and 1,900 furniture stores in Saudi Arabia. 500 Turkish-operated businesses are functioning in Kuwait and 600 in Libya, specializing in trades such as car repairs, painting, hair dressing, construction, upholstery, furniture making, carpentry, jewelry, and dress making (Anatolia News Agency, 6/11/1999; *Skylife*, May 2001).

LIVING STANDARDS

Household Spending: According to the 1994 study on household income and consumption patterns conducted by the State Planning Organization (SPO), Turkish households spend 36% of their income on food (up to 49% in urban areas and down to 31% in rural areas); 23% on housing; 9% on clothing, transportation, and furniture; 2.6% on health; 1.4% on education; and 3% on recreation. Another study shows that in Istanbul, households spend 27% of their income on food, 25% on rent, 12% on clothing, 11% on housing, 10% on transportation and communication, 5% on cultural activities and entertainment, 4% on eating out, 4% on health and personal care, and the remaining 2% on other expenditures (*AC Nielsen Zet* 1997). 86% of Istanbul residents use local market places where vendors sell their own produce. 76% use ATM cards and 38% use credit cards. (Prof. Emre Kongar, *Life Style and Problems of Istanbul Population,* a study conducted for the Istanbul Chamber of Commerce, 2000.)

Living Standards: 97.4% of households have refrigerators, 96.6% have television sets, 92.5% have irons, and 79% have washing machines. 96.2% of households do not have personal computers, 91.9% do not have VCRs, and 85.5% do not have dishwashers. 22.4% of households in the Marmara region (Istanbul and environs) have dishwashers as compared with 3.9% in the southeast. 5.4% of households in the Marmara region have personal computers as compared with 1.2% in the southeast. *(Forum,* May 2000.) 36% of the urban households in the top income group have normal and 70% have "no frost" refrigerators as compared with 81% and 9% respectively for the households in the lowest income group. 10% of urban families in the lowest income group do not have refrigerators. 20% of urban households in the top income group have VCR and DVD players as compared with none in the lowest income group. (VERI ARASTIRMA A.S., *Kentsel Turkiye Raporu, Report on Urban Turkey.)* According to another more recent study, 98% of Istanbul households own refrigerators, 96% own television sets and washing machines, 92% own ovens, 75% own dishwashers, and 14% own personal computers (Prof Emre Kongar, *Life Style and Problems of Istanbul Population,* a study conducted for the Istanbul Chamber of Commerce, 2000).

House Ownership: According to a study conducted by the State Institute of Studies (SIS) in 1991, 71% of households own the residence where the household is living, 22% pay rent, and 3% live in government or company housing. 11.5% of Turks own second homes (Piar-Gallup, *Cumhuriyet,* June 10, 1998). 84% of Istanbul residents live in apartments (Prof. Emre Kongar, *Life Style and Problems of Istanbul Population,* a study conducted for the Istanbul Chamber of Commerce, 2000). This figure would be typical for many urban centers.

According to the SIS (1990), there are bathrooms in 97% of all houses (69% according to the 1989 Association of Turkish Industrialists and Businessmen-TUSIAD study) and kitchens in 91% of all houses (81% according to the 1989 TUSIAD study). Again, according to the SIS (1990), 99.3% of all houses have electricity and 77.5% (69% according to 1989 TUSIAD study) have running water.

Car Ownership: Car ownership increased 27 times over the last 2 decades. Despite the increase, car ownership in Turkey remains relatively low at 102 cars per 1000. 72.3% of Turks does not have a driver's license. (Piar Gallup, *Cumhuriyet,* June 10, 1998.) According to "Report on Urban Turkey" by VERI ARASTIRMA A.S., urban households in the top income group (10% of total population) have 135 cars per 100 households as compared with 2 per 100 households in the lowest income group (45% of total population). 40% of Istanbul households own cars. (Prof Emre Kongar, *Life Style and Problems of Istanbul Population,* a study conducted for the Istanbul Chamber of Commerce, 2000.)

36% of cars used in Turkey are produced by Turkish Fiat, 31% by Turkish Renault, 10% by Turkish Ford, and 3% by Mercedes Benz. 40%

of Istanbul residents own cars. 25% of all cars in Turkey are in Istanbul, 14.1% in Ankara, 7.5% in Izmir, 4% in Bursa, 3.5% in Antalya, and 3.2% in Adana.

Cities where motorcycles are used most densely are Antalya, Adana, Izmir, and Konya. Motorcycles are not very popular in Istanbul, probably because the city is hilly and the areas where low-income people (who would use motorcycles) live are located away from major centers.

CAR OWNERSHIP IN TURKEY AND IN SELECTED COUNTRIES	
Country	Cars/1000 Persons
France	545
Germany	512
Italy	425
EU Average	394
UK	366
Portugal	227
Greece	176
Turkey	102
World Average	86

COMMUNICATIONS

The Telephone Network: The telephone network is owned and run by the government-owned company Turk Telekom. For privatization purposes, Telekom was separated from the government-owned PTT, which also runs the postal services. Over the previous decade, Telekom invested 80% of its revenues. This percentage is the highest among the telecommunications companies of Eastern Europe. Consequently, there has been a major improvement in Turkey's telephone network. The telephone network is digital, and automatic telephone links exist throughout Turkey and between Turkey and the rest of the world. The number of telephone users is expected to rise from 19.150 million to 19.650 by the end of 2002. (*Milliyet.com.tr,* 05/11/2001.)

There are two cellular networks, one in the form of an analog and the other in the form of a digital cellular system. The analog system, used mainly in motor vehicles, is shrinking. Subscribers to the analog system dropped 92 thousand to 55 thousand in 2001. This

TELEPHONE OWNERSHIP IN SELECTED COUNTRIES	
Country	Number of Telephones per 100 Persons
Average for OECD Countries	63
EU Average	52
Greece	50
Portugal	30
Turkey	32
World Average	13
Average for FormerEast Bloc Countries	11
Average for Developing Countries	2.6

figure is expected to fall to 40,000 in 2002. The number of digital cellular subscribers was 17 million at the end of 2001 and this figure is expected to reach 20 million by the end of 2002. (Milliyet.com.tr, 05/11/2001.)

Radio and Television: Until recently, radio and TV production was a state monopoly. Turkish companies first broke this monopoly by broadcasting from abroad via satellite. Today, there are roughly 20 national and 260 local private TV channels and 1,065 private radio stations (*Hürriyet,* July 28, 1999). 29 TV channels and 128 radio stations are based in Istanbul. The Ankara-and-Istanbul-based government radio-and-television network TRT (Turkish Radio and Television) operates five TV channels and several radio stations. At the end of 2000, there were 885,000 subscribers to the cable TV provided by Telekom. (*Milliyet.com.tr,* 05/11/2001.)

Newspapers: The total number of periodicals is 3,500. 964 of these are based in Istanbul (*Hürriyet,* July 28, 1999). 400 daily newspapers are published. The total daily circulation of newspapers reaches 4 million; the average is 64 daily newspapers per 1000 persons per day. This figure is about one tenth to one fifth of the averages in the West. According to a recent poll, 32.2% of the population reads newspapers, 12.1% reads weekly periodicals, and 6.6% reads monthly periodicals regularly (Piar-Gallup, *Radikal,* June 9, 1998). 59% of households do not buy newspapers and 88% do not buy weekly periodicals. 50% of the newspapers and periodicals published in Turkey are sold in Istanbul. 40% of Istanbul residents read newspapers regularly. (Tufan Turenc, *Hürriyet,* December 22.)

Internet Use: Turkey is 41st among world nations in terms of Internet usage (*Hürriyet,* January 24, 1999). There were 4 million Internet users in Turkey at the end of 2001, and this number was expected to rise to 6 million by the end of 2002 (*Milliyet.com.tr,* 5/11/2001). 54% of Turkish Internet users connect to the World Wide Web through computers at home, 26% through their offices, 26% through Internet cafes, and 10% through their friends' computers. There are 23 PCs and 0.73 internet connections per 1000. (*UN Development Report, 2000.*) Most Turkish internet users utilize the medium to make inquiries about potential purchases rather than to actually buy things. The total volume of "e-business" in Turkey is estimated as $15–20 million. According to the Economist Intelligence Unit, Turkey ranks 39th in the world, below Greece and above India, Russia, and China in terms of its potential for e-business.

TRANSPORTATION

Railways: During the early years of the Republic, the government placed great emphasis on the construction of railways. However, after the Second World War, emphasis has been on highways and railways have been neglected. The length of railways constructed since 1950 is only 788 km. The total length of railways is 8,452 km. Turkey's railways are the 25th longest in the world, whereas Turkey's highways are the 13th longest.

Only 8.1% (1033 km) of railways are electrified compared with 82% in developed countries. 98% of railways are single lane and 44% are in need of repairs. The fastest speed that can be realized by Turkish trains is 120 km/hour, and the fastest average speed attained on the Istanbul-Ankara route is 80 km/hour.

Only 4% of the passengers (24% in 1955) and 7% of cargo are carried by railways. 80% of passenger traffic on railways is on local trains, compared with 15% in the EU and 41% in the USA. One reason why highways are preferred to railways in goods shipment is because of the continued employment of old-style freight cars weighing 33 tons each, which increases the unit costs in railway transportation. If the average weight of railway cars were to be reduced to the world average of 17 tons, Turkey's total annual energy savings would be equivalent to the amount of energy that is annually being produced by the Ataturk Dam.

Railways are run by the government-owned Company State Railways (DDY). Annual losses of the DDY are about 850 million dollars. A World Bank report (1996) estimates that over the next 5 years DDY will need 450 million dollars in government subsidies, will defer the payment of 570 million dollars worth of social security benefits, and will require 1.5 billion dollars worth of new credit.

Highways: The total length of highways is 320,000 km, of which 30,000 km are paved (5,000 km asphalt) and 1,765 km are expressways. 72% of all transportation is conducted on highways. This ratio is 10% in the European countries and 12% in the USA. There are 450,000 trucks in Turkey. This is equal to the total number of trucks in 14 European countries. 15% of all cars, 70% of all minibuses, 73% of all busses, and 85% of all trucks are used commercially. The number of commercial vehicles is 700,000. This means that nearly 15% of the families in Turkey are dependent on income generated on highways.

Traffic Accidents: Following the implementation of strict new laws, during the first six months of 2001, as compared with the same period in 2000, there was a 9.61% drop in traffic accidents. The number killed dropped by 21.52% and number wounded dropped by 14.11%. (*Sabah*, 23/7/2001.) There had been a 30% drop in bus accidents in 2000.

Traffic accidents are the cause of 2% of all deaths in the country, taking about 9,000 lives annually. Turkey is eighth in the world in terms of wounded per hundred million vehicles/km (*The Economist*, "World in Figures 2001"). The total number killed in traffic accidents during the last decade is 100,000. 10 times the number killed are wounded in traffic accidents. Annually, 143 out of every million die in traffic accidents. This ratio is 79 in Finland, 76 in Holland, 64 in Britain, 61 in Sweden, and 115 for the EU as a whole. People injured or killed per thousand vehicles is 25 in Turkey, 31 in Israel, 26 in South Africa, 17 in the US, 16 in Egypt, 13 in the UK, 12 in Germany, 14 in Canada, 10 in Greece, 9 in New Zealand, 8 in Italy, and 6 in France (World Bank).

Navigation: Turkish ships handle 29% of exports and 34% of imports. There are 1,279 ships in the merchant navy, 8% of which are tankers. The Turkish merchant marine has grown by 250% during the last decade. The growth was financed through annual credits of 1.5 to 2 billion dollars supplied by international banks. The size of the fleet is roughly 10 million dead weight tons (DWT). The present size of Greek fleet is 185 million DWT. The primary problem facing the merchant fleet is its age. Average age of ships is 20 years. Shipbuilding capacity growth has paralleled the growth of the maritime marine. Present annual shipbuilding capacity is 500,000 DWT. Yachts worth $20 million dollars are exported annually.

Air Transportation: The government-owned Turkish Airlines (THY) is the largest airline operator in Turkey. There are also 9 private companies that operate flights on international and domestic routes. THY flies to a total of 113 domestic and international destinations; it controls 85% of the domestic and 20% of the international air-passenger traffic. Turkish-owned private companies control 15% of domestic and 37% of international air-passenger traffic. Foreign-owned airlines control 43% of Turkey's international air-passenger traffic.

The number of passengers carried by the THY increased by 1 million annually during the previous decade. THY has doubled the size of its fleet since 1991, bringing the total number to 68. The average age of its jets was 6.2 as of 2002, which made the THY one of the youngest fleets in Europe. With its seat capacity of 10,855, THY is the 43rd largest airline in the world and 9th largest in Europe.

There are 15 civilian airports. The new international building at the Istanbul Ataturk airport can handle 14 million passengers. The previous international building at the same airport, which was built to handle 4 million a year, handled 10 million in 1997.

GOVERNMENT

Central Government: Turkey is a parliamentary democracy like Canada, Australia, New Zealand, Germany, and Israel; it has a parliament, a prime minister, and a head of state, the president elected by parliament. The cabinet headed by the prime minister handles government affairs. By convention, the president appoints the leader of the largest party represented in the parliament as the prime minister. In order to rule, the government needs a vote of confidence by the parliament.

The president rules but does not govern. In theory an apolitical office, the president has some executive powers. He or she heads the National Security Council, a powerful consultative body that monthly brings together top military with key ministers and the prime minister. The president also makes direct appointments to some top-level judgeships and to the Council on Higher Education. Presidents of government-owned universities are appointed by the president from amongst the candidates suggested by the Higher Education Council. The laws passed by the parliament are promulgated by the president within 15 days. The president may refer the law back to the parliament for reconsideration.

The parliament legislates; supervises the Council of Ministers; adopts the budget; and decides on war and the deployment of troops abroad, and on martial law and on emergency rule. International agreements, general or special amnesties, and the death penalty need to be approved by the parliament.

The parliament is unicameral and has 550 seats. Elections for the parliament are held every six years. The parliament and the president can decide to hold new elections before the six-year term is completed. An intermediary election is held only if 5% of the total number of seats are vacated due to death, resignation, etc. Once elected, MPs receive immunity from prosecution, unless the immunity is lifted by the parliament.

The president is elected by the parliament. A presidential candidate does not need to be a member of the parliament. The presidential term is seven years. The president cannot be re-elected. The president in 2002 was Ahmet Necdet Sezer, who succeeded Suleyman Demirel in 2000. Ahmet Necdet Sezer was the president of the Constitutional Court when he was elected president.

Local Government: Turkey is divided into 78 provinces, which are administered by governors who act as representatives of the central government in Ankara. Governors are appointed by the central government and are in charge of activities run by the central government such as health, education, and security. Each province is divided into smaller units, also administered by officials *(kaymakam)* appointed by the central government. These officials are attached to the governor of their respective province.

Each town also has a municipal organization run by a mayor and a council. There are sixteen large metropolitan municipalities, with subdivisions, and 3,200 smaller townships. Municipal organizations are elected every five years and are in charge of activities such as road construction, public transportation, water supplies, sewage systems, and city planning. The governor is the highest civic authority in the province, even though his sphere of activity is different. At the village level, the elected village headman and the village council of elders also represent the central government. There are 50,000 villages.

Elections and Voter Preferences: The election system is based on proportional representation. In order to be represented in the parliament, political parties need to get at least 10% of the national vote. MPs are elected from a party list, drawn up by the virtually absolute discretionary power of party leaders. Two right-of-center parties, True Path and Motherland, are represented in the parliament. The religious conservative Welfare Party and the nationalist Movement Party are also represented. Because it failed to receive the minimum 10% vote, one of the two larger social-democrat parties, the Social Democrat People's Party, was left out of the parliament following the 1999 national elections. The other social-democrat party, Democratic Left, is represented in the parliament and their leader, Bulent Ecevit, was the leader of the coalition government formed after the elections held in 1999.

3.9% of the eligible voters are political party members and 42.5% of voters regard themselves as "progressive," 9.4% as "ultra progressive," and 9.3% as ultra conservative (Piar-Gallup, *Cumhüriyet,* June 10, 1998). According to another public-opinion poll, 27% of the population regard themselves as left wing, 51% as right wing, and 22% as centrist. If one adds moderate right and left-wingers with the centrists, centrist vote is 45%. Only 2.3% regard themselves as extreme left and 6.5% as extreme right. Left-wing tendencies seem to be correlated with level of education. 56% of the illiterate consider themselves "right wing" and 41% of those who hold graduate degrees consider themselves "left wing." 19% of the religious conservative (Welfare Party) vote is illiterate and only 7% are university graduates. (A&G Research Company, *Hürriyet,* May 19, 1999.) A quarter of the nationalist (Movement Party) vote is in the 18–28 age group and 75% is male. Half of nationalist voters live in the central or Black Sea regions and half live in towns with population less than 20,000 *(Radikal,* April 19, 1999).

At the beginning of 1997, the country was governed by a coalition of the religious conservative Welfare Party and the right-of-center True Path Party. The head of the Welfare Party, Mr. Necmettin Erbakan, was the prime minister, and the head of the True Path Party, the former prime minister, Mrs. Tansu Ciller, was the deputy prime minister. This coalition collapsed following a dispute about the extension of elementary education to eight years and a new coalition of Motherland Party and Democratic Left Party was formed. The country went to elections on April 18, 1999, under a Democratic Left minority government. Following the 1999 elections, the Democratic Left, the Motherland, and the Nationalist Movement Parties formed a coalition government. Prime Minister Mr. Bulent Ecevit, leader of the Democratic Left Party, also was the prime minister during Turkey's military intervention in Cyprus in 1974.

VOTER PREFERENCES (%)			
	1994 Local Elections	1995 General Elections	1999 General Elections
Right Wing Parties			
True Path	20	19.65	12.01
Motherland	20	19.18	13.22
Welfare	19	21.38	15.41
National Movement	8	8.18	17.98
Left Wing Parties			
Social Democratic People's	13	10.71	8.71
Democratic Left	12	14.64	22.19

THE MILITARY

Men who reach the age of 20 serve in the armed forces for 18 months. Military service can be postponed until the completion of post-secondary education. Officers are professionals. Only 17% of the military is made up of professionals. College graduates have the option to serve as sublieutenants for 18 months or as privates for 9 months. Turkish youths who live and work abroad serve for only 2 months and make a payment as compensation. Military service is not obligatory for women. There are professional women officers in the services.

There are roughly 800,000 soldiers in the Turkish armed forces. In terms of manpower, this is sixth largest standing armed force in the world. The armed forces are made up four branches: the army, navy, air force, and gendarmerie. The army has 3,445 tanks (the fifth-largest tank force in the world) and 5,000 armored personnel carriers. The backbone of the air force is F-16 jets assembled in Turkey. F-5s and Phantoms are also in use. The navy has 11 destroyers, 21 frigates, 16 submarines (the ninth-largest submarine fleet in the world), and 48 gunboats. The gendarmerie is in charge of security in the countryside; in this capacity they are attached to the Interior Ministry.

It is estimated that Turkey purchases one-sixth of all arms traded in the international market annually *(Ekonomist,* Dec 27, 1998). During 1990–1995, Turkey spent $8 billion dollars on arms imports, which made it the biggest arms importer in the world during that period. The USA supplies one-third of the arms sold to Turkey. France, Germany, Israel, Italy, Holland, Romania, and Russia are the other major suppliers. *(Gazete Pazar,* March 16, 1997.)

Turkey spends $10 per square kilometer to defend its land, compared with Greece, which spends $43. In terms of percentage of national income spent on the military, Turkey is the 22nd in the world. *(1999 CIA World Factbook.)* Annually, approximately 4.3% of the national income is spent on military expenditures, compared with 2.53% on education. This is slightly lower than the world average of 6.1% (9% in Armenia, 8% in Syria, 7% in the UK, and 5% in Greece). Defense expenditures make up 20% of the budget, compared with 1.3% in New Zealand, 2.2% in South Africa, 2.5% in Australia, 1.7% in Canada, 3% in the UK, 3.8% in the US, 5.5% in Greece, and 9.6% in Israel. 8% of the budget is spent on education, 2% on health, and less than 1% on culture. In terms of total expenditures on the military, Turkey was 17th in the world in 1999 with per-capita expenditures of $6,737, right after Australia, which had per-capita expenditures of $6,900. *(1999 CIA World Factbook.)*

The military is engaged in a modernization project that involves the purchase of 145 attack helicopters, 1000 tanks, 7 Awacs, 30 reconnaissance planes, and 6 navy patrol planes. The newly purchased tanks will be so-called "third-generation" models and will be used to replace the "second-generation" models currently used by Turkey.

Arms Imports in 1990–1995	
Country	Arms Imports ($)
Turkey	8,096,000,000
Egypt	7,138,000,000
Saudi Arabia	7,092,000,000
Japan	6,882,000,000
Greece	5,756,000,000
India	5,158,000,000
China	4,747,000,000
Israel	4,293,000,000
Taiwan	4,228,000,000
Germany	4,045,000,000

The delivery of tanks is to take place over 2004–2013. The first group of 250 will be built by 2008.

PKK TERRORISM

The Kurds live in four countries: Turkey, Iraq, Iran, and Syria. The total estimated population of Kurds is 25 million. Half of the Kurds live in Turkey, and half of those living in Turkey have one non-Kurdish parent. This would imply that about 20% of the population of Turkey is of Kurdish origin (10% with one Kurdish parent only). However, both according to the results of the censuses held between 1927–1965 (Sukru Elekdag, *Milliyet* June 14, 1999), which recorded ethnic origins of those polled, and according to a study conducted by Prof. Ahmet Yucekok in 1993 (*Milliyet* February 27, 1993), those who regard themselves as "Kurdish" are no more than 7% of the population. In general, Kurdish identity is correlated with lower income and education levels. 13.3% of Istanbul population over nineteen have Kurdish parental or marital bonds, yet only 29.3% of this population regard themselves as "Kurdish." 27.8% regard themselves as "Kurdish-Turkish" and 42.85% as "Turkish." The tendency to regard oneself as "Turkish" rises with the level of education. The percentage of those who have post-graduate degrees is twice as high among those who regard themselves as "Kurdish-Turks" as compared with those who regard themselves as purely "Kurdish." The education level of those who regard themselves as "Turkish" despite their Kurdish bonds is higher than both other groups and higher than the average level of education in Turkey. (Prof. Ahmet Yucekok, *Milliyet* February 27, 1993)

There has never been a Kurdish state. Traditionally, Kurds are a tribal and mountain people. Kurdish nationalists claim descent from the ancient peoples of the Middle East, such as the Meds. Other historians have claimed that the Kurds originated amongst the Indo-Europeans of the Indus Valley region. Historical evidence to verify these claims is rather flimsy. According to another view, Kurds are a Turkic people, descendants of the Scythians, speaking a dialect of the Turkish language that is permeated by the languages of neighboring Iran and Iraq. There are 532 words that were inscribed on the eighth-century Turkish monuments at Orhun in central Asia but are not used in modern Turkish that are in use in Kurdish dialects. Kurdish dialects are similar to Turkish in terms of morphology and phenomenology. The word order is like the Turkish word order. 3,000 of the 8,528 words in the Kurdish dictionary compiled by the St. Petersburg Academy are Turkish. (A. Taner Kislali, *Cumhuriyet*, October 18, 1992.)

According to the Japanese linguist Goishi Kojima, the Kurds speak ten different dialects that are mutually incomprehensible and the "Kurdish" spoken by people changes at every 40–50 km in southeast Turkey. The main dialects spoken in Turkey are Kirmanch and Zaza. That Kurdish is not sufficient to meet basic communication needs of people and for cultural development had been acknowledged by Kurdish nationalists such as Mehmet Sukru Sekban, as early as 1908 (Sukru Elekdag, *Milliyet* June 28, 1999).

The Turkish constitution bans discrimination amongst citizens based on ethnic, religious, class, or gender differences. There is no discrimination against Kurdish subjects. Government and military positions are open to all. Intermarriage is accepted and widespread. Kurds vote; Kurds are elected to office; and they live in the region, city, and neighborhood of their own choice. Half the Kurds in Turkey live in the east and southeast, and the other half are spread throughout the rest of the country.

During the previous decade, the PKK (Workers' Party of Kurdistan) waged a guerrilla campaign in southeast Turkey with rather vague aims. Their stand continuously shifted during this period, at times demanding "cultural rights" or, at other times, outright independence. Their methods were ruthless (reminiscent of Pol Pot and Khmer Rouge) such as exterminating all villagers, including newborn babies, if the village adults failed to give them adequate support.

Several authorities believe that what bred PKK terrorism was social and economic inequality. 92% of the large farms in Turkey (larger than 2500 decars) are in the southeast. 80% of land in the southeast is owned by 5% of population. 50% of farmers in the area own no land. 20% of the population own land that is sufficient for subsistence only. The situation is worsened by the fact that families in the area have the highest fertility rates in Turkey. The average fertility of women is 2 in the west and 4.2 in the east and southeast. Unemployment among youth is up to 90% in some towns in the southeast.

The PKK received support from some of Turkey's neighbors. In 1995, members of Greek Parliament headed by deputy speaker of the parliament Mr. Panayotis Sguridis visited the PKK headquarters in the Bekaa Valley (*Milliyet* July 1, 1995). In 1997, high-level PKK officials were entertained in Athens by certain members of the Greek parliament. In June 1997, it was disclosed in the Greek Cypriot press that retired Greek admiral Naksakis trained PKK terrorists. Several PKK activists have confessed to receiving their training in Greece (*Time,* April 4, 1998). Such allegations were also affirmed by Nicholas Burns, US Ambassador to Greece (*Milliyet* June 20, 1999).

Syria was by far the most important supporter of the PKK, providing it with bases in the parts of Bekaa Valley under its control and providing its leader Apo with a home and headquarters in Damascus. In 1998, Turkey put strong pressure on Syria to end such support. As a result, Apo was forced to leave Syria, and he moved to Italy. He was forced to leave Italy under pressure from Turkey; he was eventually arrested in Kenya and brought to Turkey for trial. During his stay in Kenya, Apo was in hiding at the residence of the Greek Ambassador in Nairobi.

PKK made most of its money from drugs. It was estimated that 60 tons of opium and hashish were grown in the parts of the Bekaa Valley controlled by the PKK. Drugs from Lebanon and Pakistan are distributed in Europe through families of the "Kurdish Mafia." The organization has more than 300 alleged sympathy groups worldwide that are also involved in the dealings. The annual income the PKK derived from drug dealing was estimated to be around $50 million (*Cumhuriyet*, January 15, 1999). That PKK was involved in drug dealing was exposed in the Panorama program of the German Television ARD. The program had interviews with those who were living in luxurious villas even though they had no apparent income other than social security. A drug production workshop in Hamburg, which supplied drugs to different parts of Germany for six years, was controlled directly by the PKK (*Milliyet* July 8, 1999). Another source of income for the organization was the fees derived through extortion from the Kurdish refugees in Europe. The organization bought loyalty using its immense wealth.

The Turkish security forces waged a strong campaign against the PKK. The bases of the organization in northern Iraq were hit and greatly damaged on several occasions. Currently, the PKK reign of terror is all but finished. It is expected that the problem will be ultimately eliminated through the implementation of the Southeast Anatolia Project, which will thoroughly transform the social and economic structure in the area. The campaign against the PKK will have cost Turkey and the people of the area dearly. The total cost of the 14 years campaign is estimated around $84 billion. This amount would have been sufficient to complete not one but three Southeast Anatolia Projects.

As for Apo, the leader of the terrorist organization, he has been sentenced to death following his trial by a Turkish court. The penalty is pending approval by the Turkish parliament. Under Turkish law, all death penalties need to be approved by the parliament and the president. None has been put on the agenda of the parliament for the last twenty years. In Apo's case, the government has chosen to wait for the decision of the European Human Rights court on Apo's appeal, in which he objects to the circumstances of his arrest when leaving the

Greek Embassy Residence in Nairobi, before asking the parliament to debate his conviction. As part of the process to join the EU, Turkey may abolish the death penalty before the Human Rights Court reaches a verdict on the appeal. In the meantime, Apo is proving himself useful in the hands of government authorities. He had stated that he would "cooperate" as soon as he was arrested and has his since declared the futility of military conflict and reduced the aims of his struggle to the recognition of Kurdish identity and Kurdish language within the boundaries of the unitary Turkish State.

INTERNATIONAL POLICY AND RELATIONS WITH NEIGHBORS

Foreign Policy Principles: Turkey's international policy follows the vision of Ataturk, founder of the Republic, summarized in the statement "Peace at home, peace in the world," meaning that only self defense is justified. In this very turbulent part of the world, Turkey has refrained from all wars since the founding of the Republic in 1923, including the Second World War. The peace this land has enjoyed under the Turkish Republic is probably the longest in its very ancient history. Turkey has been a member of NATO since 1951.

Relations with Russia: The Russian Bolsheviks were the only government that provided Turkish nationalists with some help during the War of Independence. Relations were friendly between the two countries until after the Second World War when Stalin demanded Turkey's eastern provinces and a control over the Straits. Turkey resisted these demands on her own, while seeking NATO membership. Cold War years between the two countries ended with a détente, which started in 1963. During the following decade the Soviets financed and built several heavy industry projects in Turkey, including a refinery, a steel mill, a copper smelter, and an aluminum plant. Trade ties have intensified since the dissolution of the Soviet Union. Turkish contractors build extensively in Russia, and Turkey has made agreements to buy large amounts of natural gas from Russia.

Relations With Israel: Turkey established diplomatic relations with Israel in 1949 and for three decades remained the only Muslim country to recognize Israel. The friendly relations between Turkey and Israel are dictated by overlapping security, political, and economic interests. The two nations share concerns about religious fundamentalism, terrorism, illicit drugs, and arms trafficking, as well as the proliferation of weapons of mass destruction, including nuclear weapons. Leaders of the two nations emphasize that they are bound together by their commitment to democracy and free trade; they repeat that their relations are not directed against any other state. The Jewish community in Turkey, which is made up of the descendants of the Morano Jews rescued from the Inquisition in Spain by the Ottoman sultan in 1492 and the descendants of the Central European Jews who fled from persecution in Central Europe to the Ottoman realm, has functioned as a bridge of friendship between the two nations. Turkish Jews celebrated the year 1992, as the "qui centennial" of their arrival from Spain, Turkey being the only land where they have lived in peace for the past five hundred years.

Turkey and Israel have shared a free-trade agreement since 1996. Non-military trade has increased from a very low level to nearly a billion dollars a year over the past decade. The two nations have set a target of doubling their two-way trade to $2 billion. Israeli tourists numbering 250,000–300,000 have visited Turkey each year since the mid-1990s, helping to strengthen people-to-people ties. Turkey may become an important source of water for Israel. Effective means are being sought to bring water from Manavgat in southern Turkey to Israel.

A military cooperation pact between Israel and Turkey was signed in 1996. The two navies and air forces have joint training exercises, and pilots of either country use one another's airspace. The aged F-4 and F-5 fighter jets of the Turkish air force and aged M-60 tanks of the Turkish army are being modernized by Israel. Israeli firms are in the running to sell an early warning system to Turkey and to manufacture 1,000 tanks and 1,000 helicopters. The two countries have an agreement to jointly produce the Popeye missile, with a range of about 150 kilometers.

Israel was one of the first countries to respond to Turkey's earthquake in August 1999. Israel sent a 250-member rescue team, established a large field hospital in Duzce with 100 doctors, nurses, medics, and administrative personnel, and collected and sent over 200 tons of goods—including clothes, blankets, toys, medicine, food, and hygiene products to Turkey. Israel built a prefabricated village, including a school and playground, to house 2,500 people who lost their homes.

Relations With Palestine: While maintaining close and friendly relations with Israel, Turkey has always recognized the right of Palestinians for self determination. Turkey has always defended the view that a fair and just solution to the problem in the region is the founding of the State of Palestine on the West Bank. The excessive use of force in Palestine in Spring 2002 was openly criticized by the Turkish government.

Relations with Iraq: Turkey was the first country to start the UN embargo against Iraq by closing down the pipeline that linked the oil fields in Musul to the Turkish port of Ceyhan. Even though Turkey did not participate in the Gulf War, allied planes used bases in Turkey. Allied planes that patrolled Iraq after the Gulf war also continued to fly out of Turkey.

Relations with Iran: Turkey's border with Iran has not changed since the seventeenth century. Yet the two countries have always been rivals for leadership and influence in the Middle East. Since the Islamic revolution in Iran, Turkey has accused Iran of trying to export its revolution to Turkey, and Iran has blamed Turkey for giving shelter to counter revolutionaries. Turkey also accuses Iran of sheltering Kurdish PKK leaders and guerillas. In the meantime, trade is developing. Turkey has signed a bill to purchase a total of $23 billion worth of natural gas from Iran.

Relations with Syria: The thorny issue between Damascus and Ankara is the Syrian territorial claim over the Turkish province of Hatay, the old sancak of Alexandretta. The province, which was under French control after the First World War, was not initially part of the territory of the Turkish Republic. In 1936 the French granted Syria its independence and planned to give it Alexandretta, but Turkey's opposition brought the problem in front of the League of Nations, which concluded that Turks were a majority in the province. Elections produced a local parliament with a Turkish majority, which promptly declared an independent Hatay republic in 1938 and a year later, on 27 July 1939, the new state announced its union with Turkey, much to the chagrin of Syria, which never accepted the decision. To this day, some Syrian maps still include the province of Hatay.

THE GAP PROJECT AND TURKEY'S NEIGHBORS

The implementation of the Southeast Anatolia Project (GAP) has created tensions between Turkey and her Arab neighbors. Annually, the Euphrates carries 30 million cubic meters of water to Syria, meeting 90% of this country's needs. According to one estimate, the full implementation of the GAP scheme, including the irrigation projects, will cut Syria's permanent share of the Euphrates by 40% and Iraq's by 80% (Estimate by Prof. Thomas Naff of the University of Pennsylvania, *Economist*, May 12, 1990). Because of its high population growth rate of 3.8% per year, the highest in the Middle East, Syria may have water shortage problems even if the supply from the Euphrates is not reduced.

Iraq and Syria claim that the Euphrates and Tigris are international and shared resources; and that they have "acquired rights" over the Euphrates related to "ancestral irrigation" dating from ancient Sumerian periods. They say that Turkey, an upstream state, has no right to take away these rights; and they demand the sharing of waters according to the needs that each country will determine separately.

Turkey claims, however, that the demands of Syria and Iraq lack good will, are unrealistic, and are exaggerated.

Turkey says that joint Syrian and Iraqi claims on the Euphrates lack good will because they do not take into consideration the waters of the Tigris, which flows from Turkey into Iraq, whereas the Euphrates flows first into Syria and then into Iraq. Turkey can use only 13% of the waters of Tigris although 51% of it originates on its soil. If Iraq were to channel some of the waters of the Tigris to the Euphrates using the Thartar canal near Baghdad, its demands on the Euphrates would be greatly reduced. Another sign of the lack of good will on behalf of these Arab states is Syria's allowing only 10% of the waters of the river Orontes, which originates on its soil, to flow into Turkey.

Syrian and Iraqi claims are unrealistic because the water demanded by Syria and Iraq exceeds the total capacity of the river. Total water flow on the Euphrates is 35 billion cubic meters, 89% of which originates in Turkey. Turkey wishes to use 51% (18 billion cubic meters) of the waters of the Euphrates. Syria, where 11% (4 billion cubic meters) of the waters of the Euphrates originate, wishes to use 35% of the total (12 billion cubic meters) and Iraq, where none of the waters of the river originates, claims 66% (23 billion cubic meters) of the total.

Finally, Syrian and Iraqi claims are exaggerated. Syrian farmers use the archaic flooding technique in irrigation, which wastes 70% of the water. Syria's water needs would be greatly reduced if more modern irrigation methods were employed.

In response to the Syrian-Iraqi proposals outlined above, Turkey proposes a three-stage plan. This plan involves an inventory study of water resources in the three countries including a study of evaporation, temperature and rainfall; an inventory study of land resources based on soil classification and of irrigation methods; and allocation of water on the basis of irrigation and leaching water requirements based on the above information and on the assumption that projects that minimize water losses are employed.

In order to fill the Ataturk dam completely at the outset, Turkey would have had to stop the Euphrates for nearly two years. In practice, the filling has been gradual. Turkey has further demonstrated her good will by providing Syria with 500 cubic meters of water per second from the Euphrates. Syria would like this amount to be raised to 700 cubic meters per second and for Turkey to make a formal commitment to this end.

Turkey claims that the construction of the dams on the Euphrates is a blessing and not a problem for Syria. The dams assure a regular supply of water rather than wet and dry seasons. In 1989 the existence of dams enabled Turkey to maintain the flow of 500 cubic meters per second even though the flow of the river had dropped to 289 cubic meters per second.

There is concern that Turkey may be subjected to international pressures to give concessions with regard to water as part of a peace deal in the Middle East. 15% of the total water consumption for Israel is from the Golan Heights. Israel wishes to continue to use this water source even if the area were to be returned to Syria.

However, the idea that Turkey is "water-rich" enough to donate water to her neighbors is an illusion. The country can hardly rank in the same league as Canada or New Zealand, where the amount of water per capita is over 100,000 cubic meters. Water resources per capita are 1,420 cubic meters in Syria, 2,110 cubic meters in Iraq, and 1,830 cubic meters in Turkey. Turkey's total water potential is 186 billion cubic meters, of which only 110 billion cubic meters is available. Turkey utilizes only 26 billion cubic meters of its capacity. The remaining 84 billion cubic meters is not surplus but represents the amount that cannot yet be allocated to the country's needs. In the year 2020, if Turkey cannot find a better means of utilizing its water resources, the amount of water available per capita will be down to 980 cubic meters.

Nevertheless, Turkey has developed projects that would considerably contribute to the water needs of her neighbors. A "peace pipeline," which could carry 6 million cubic meters of the waters of the rivers Seyhan and Ceyhan to Syria, Iraq, Jordan, Saudi Arabia, and to the Gulf, has been rejected by Arab states as a propaganda ploy. The project involves two pipelines, one reaching Jeddah in Saudi Arabia and the other reaching the Gulf. The estimated cost of the project is 21 billion dollars, and the estimated cost of water to be provided by the project is $1 per cubic meter. Turkey has also completed a project that enables her to sell 500,000 cubic meters of the waters of the Manavgat River daily to the water-needy countries of North Africa and the Middle East.

CENTRAL ASIA, OIL, STRAITS

Relations with Central Asian Republics: Turkey has friendly relations with the newly independent Turkic republics of Central Asia with which it shares a common heritage. Turkish companies operating in these countries invest in tourism, oil production, and textiles. Turkey's share in total direct investment in Kazakhastan, Azerbaijan, the Kyrgyz Republic, and Uzbekistan varies between 5–15%.

CENTRAL ASIAN REPUBLICS				
Country	Population (million)	Area (sq. km)	Capital City	Main Products
Uzbekistan	25,000,000	4,470,000	Tashkent	Cotton, second largest producer of gold after South Africa
Azerbaijan	7,500,000	86,600	Baku	Oil, iron, lead and cobalt
Turkmenistan	3,000,000	488,000	Ashkabat	Oil, natural gas, potassium
Kazakhastan	17,000,000	2,717,300	Alma Ata	Cotton, oil, natural gas, tin
The Kyrgyz Republic	4,400,000	198,500	Bishkek	Oil

Central Asian Oil: According to various estimates, Central Asian oil may equal 3–16% of world reserves. In 1996, the US Department of Energy experts made the rather optimistic decision that 178 billion bbl. of oil reserves may exist in the Caspian Sea—making the area second only to Saudi Arabia with 259 billion bbl. of reserves, twice the size of Kuwait's 94 billion and Iran's 93 billion. Azerbaijan's oil fields under the Caspian may contain more than 30 billion bbl. Kazakhastan fields may hold as much as 95 billion bbl. And Turkmenistan may be sitting on as much as 33 billion bbl. of oil. According to more conservative estimates, oil exports from the region will triple to 2.5 million bbl. a day in 2005 and rise again to about 3.5 million bbl. in 2010. During this period, global demand for oil is forecast to increase about 30% or 1.5 billion bbl. a day every year. Caspian exports will therefore equal no more than two years' increased supply and be equivalent in importance in 2010 to Norway's production in early 1998. *(Time,* June 29, 1998.)

One of the most heated international issues in the area is about the transportation of Central Asian oil. (It has been argued that the recent "War against Terrorism" in Afghanistan was really about transporting oil through Afghanistan to Pakistan.) Some of the oil will go to the Far East. Iran would like a pipeline through Iran to the Gulf. But this route has proved to be expensive and the US objects to this route for political reasons. Russia would like the oil to arrive at its Black Sea ports. This route involves a pipeline going through troubled Chechnya and would require the oil to be shipped through the Bosphorus and Dardanelles. Turkey opposes this plan because of the potential threats it poses to the environment, especially for Istanbul (see next section). Turkey proposes the oil reach the Mediterranean by a pipeline through Turkey. And the US wants oil to flow through many pipelines so that no single player can control the flow. Following the political will expressed by Turkey, Georgia, and Azerbaijan, the Azerbaijan oil consortium is likely to opt for a pipeline to run through Turkey, and this decision will affect what other operators will do.

Transportation of Oil, Bosphorus, and Dardanelles: The Montreux Treaty signed in 1936 recognizes the Bosphorus and the Dardanelles as Turkey's coastal waters but obliges Turkey to provide for unlimited "free and unhampered access" for all commercial navigation through the Straits. Military vessels of the Black Sea countries of Bulgaria, Romania, Ukraine, Russia, and Georgia also have free and unlimited access. Other countries can have a maximum of two navy boats for a maximum of two weeks in the Black Sea.

Navigation on both the Bosphorus and the Dardanelles can be tricky. At the Bosphorus, the less salty Black Sea flows on the surface to the south and the saltier Marmara flows at the bottom to the north. At the Dardanelles, the relatively less salty Marmara flows on the surface to the south and the saltier Aegean flowed at the bottom to the north. The reverse currents lead to several cross-currents and whirlpools. At either strait, the surface current usually runs at 3 to 4 knots, reaching 6 or 7 knots in rough weather.

The Bosphorus is very narrow and has many turns, some as sharp as 90 degrees. Because of the turns, the boats sailing on the Bosphorus need to change routes on a dozen occasions over 18 miles. Pilots regard two of these route changes as particularly difficult. The difficulty of navigation on the Bosphorus becomes clearer when one considers that it takes a loaded supertanker eight miles to stop. The Bosphorus also slopes 20 degrees from north to south, adding to the dangers and making the passage "like being in a luge." Yet, despite these difficulties, according to the Montreux Treaty, which stipulates that ships must be allowed to pass without any "formalities," Turkey cannot oblige the passing vessels to pay fees or taxes, to hire pilot services, or to rent tugboat escorts. As a result, 60% of large ships do not take local pilots. Boats passing without a pilot cause 75% of the accidents on the Bosphorus. The accident risk for boats without local pilots is 20 times as high as the risk for boats with pilots. Note that the fee for a Bosphorus pilot is $2,000, while the fee at the Suez is $135,000.

When the Montreux Treaty was signed, traffic was not as intense as it is today. Boats larger than 300 meters were not even dreamed of at the time, and boats carrying methane gas, nuclear fuel, or poisonous wastes were not known. On the first year following the signing of the treaty, the total number of boats making a passage through the straits was 2,603 with a total tonnage of 4,800,000. Since then, the annual number of boats making a passage has reached 50,000 along with thousands of ferries and small boats. The strait is already three times as busy as the Suez and four times as busy as the Panama Canal.

On the average, 135 boats pass through the straits daily. According to the Coastal Safety Chief Hucum Tulgar, "This number cannot be raised to 136." Yet Bosphorus traffic rises by 15–30% annually. The strait is also crowded with fishing vessels, cruise boats, and by commuter ferries, which make on average about 2,500 crossings each working day. 200 of these crossings are by larger ferries.

Annually 5,000 ships passing through the straits carry dangerous cargo. This number will rise to 8,000 with the operation of the Tenghiz-Novorossisk pipeline. Oil began to flow through the Tenghiz-Novorossisk pipeline in March 2001, reaching the Black Sea in June of the same year. During the initial year, 28.2 tons of oil will be transported through this pipeline; this figure is expected to reach 60 million. The total oil reserve of the Tenghiz field is estimated as 6–9 billion barrels. Currently, 44 million tons of oil goes through the straits annually. This amount will rise by 65 million tons with the operation of the Tenghiz-Novorossisk pipeline. During the years 2010–2012, 25 million tons of oil will flow in from Bulgaria and Romania, 10 million from Odessa, and 10 million from the Tuapse terminal of Russia. If the Baku-Tiblisi-Ceyhan pipeline should not be built, there will be an additional 40 billion tons of oil flowing through the straits.

During 1970–2000, 444 accidents took place on the Bosphorus. The rate of accidents is six per million transit miles—double the rate on the Suez Canal and thirty times higher than on the Mississippi River. The annual number of accidents has risen from 2 in the 1970s to 7.5 in the 1990s. Fortunately, most accidents were not significant and the dangers posed by few significant ones were avoided with good luck. If a tanker carrying 50,000 tons of liquid petroleum gas were to collide with another ship, the resulting explosion and fire could engulf an area 12 miles in diameter.

On January 11, 1994, Turkey, staying within the limits defined by the Montreux Treaty, introduced new regulations, which imposed restrictions on passage through the straits. These regulations introduced new sailing routes approved by the International Maritime Organization (IMO) and speed limits and measures that are to be taken during passage at night or in misty weather. Also, according to these regulations, boats carrying dangerous cargo are to inform the Straits Authority of their coming passage two hours beforehand. Ships longer than 200 m and/or ships carrying dangerous cargo are allowed passage only during daytime. When such a ship enters either strait at one end, the strait is closed to traffic at the other end until the passage is completed. Authorities claim that because of intense traffic, the passages of boats larger than 300 m is impossible. Since the safety regulations were imposed, the number of accidents on the Bosphorus has been reduced by 90%.

A new $20 million "Vessel Traffic Management Information System," which will provide for radar coverage to monitor the entire strait, will be in operation by the end of 2002. Seven radar stations are being set up on the Bosphorus and five on the Dardanelles. The thirty-meter-tall towers where the radars will be placed have invited protest by conservationists. The network will also be linked to the CPS satellite communications network. The system will allow boats to make a passage even in intense fog, without the guidance of lighthouses. When the system is in operation, accident risk on the straits will be reduced from the present 0.004% to, 0.00001%. (Sources: *New York Times*, January 28, 2001; Cambridge Energy Research Association; *Cumhuriyet*, 15/2/2001, 2/4/2001,20/2/2001, *Herald Tribune*, 6/4/2001.)

RELATIONS WITH ARMENIANS

Current Relations Between Turkey and the Republic of Armenia: Armenia, formerly a Soviet republic, has been Turkey's neighbor in the northeast since the dissolution of the Soviet Union. Turkey recognizes Armenia but refuses to exchange ambassadors, to open up its land borders, and to trade with this country. The reasons are manifold. Armenians worldwide are pressuring national parliaments to adopt Armenian genocide bills. The Republic of Armenia has refused to recognize the boundaries drawn between Turkey and the Soviet Union in 1921. Also, Armenia keeps under occupation 20% of Azerbaijan, a country with which Turkey has strong historical and cultural bonds, rendering one million Azerbeijani homeless. This state of affairs came about after the two countries went to war, following independence, over the Navogno Karabagh province, which was an enclave within Azerbaijan, populated by Armenians. Armenia was supported in the conflict not only by the diaspora Armenians, who provided arms, volunteers, and mercenaries, but also by the Russians, who were unhappy with the Azerbeijani who, in reaction to the bloody repression of a peaceful demonstration by Russian troops, the year before independence, would not let a Russian military presence into their country. Despite the virtual trade embargo imposed by Turkey, a large volume of Turkish goods make their way to the Armenian markets by way of Iran and Georgia. Also, there are regular flights between Istanbul and Jarevan, the capital city of Armenia.

Armenian Genocide Claims: Armenians commemorate April 24 as the day of genocide by the Ottoman government against Armenians. During the First World War, on April 24, 1915, the Ottoman government arrested 235 leaders of various Armenian organizations in the Ottoman Empire and ordered the deportation of Armenian subjects living in the eastern provinces to Lebanon, Iraq, and Syria, which were Ottoman territories at the time. These measures were taken because Armenians organized by Armenian religious and nationalist organizations had aided Russians in occupying eastern Turkey.

During the Russian occupation, atrocities were committed against Turks. The book *Armenia and the War (An Armenian's Point of View with an Appeal to Britain and the Coming Peace Conference)* by A. P. Hacopbian, (Abebooks Harfield Books of London Hodder and Stoughton, London, 1917), discusses in detail how the Armenians aided the Russians during the First World War. Boghos Nubar Pasha, who was head of the Armenian delegation at the Paris Peace Conference, which convened after the First World War, declared in his letter to the French Foreign Minister that "Armenians had fought throughout the war" [against the Turks].

When the Russian army attacked the city of Van in March 1915, Armenians in the city carried out a rebellion against the Ottoman government. On April 21, 1915, Tsar Nicholas II sent a telegram to the Armenian committee in Van that expressed his thanks for the services the committee rendered to Russia. At about the same time, the Armenian newspaper *Gochnak,* published in the USA, declared with pride that, "only 1500 Turks were left in Van." The city, which was destroyed as a result of the Armenian rebellion, now lies in ruins next to the citadel in Van. New Van was founded at its nearby location after the First World War.

The Ottoman government ordered the deportation of Armenians in eastern Turkey in response to these activities, which had cost the lives of Turkish people and endangered the security of the empire. About 700,000 Armenians living in eastern Turkey were deported by the Ottoman government and about 300,000 of those died on the way due to cold, disease, and hunger, and attacks by locals.

Armenians claim that the total number killed during the deportation was 1.5 million. This figure is highly unlikely. According to the Ottoman Census Office, which was headed by an Armenian named Migirdic, in 1915 there were only 1,294,851 Armenians living in all of the Ottoman Empire. Estimates of western consulates concerning the Armenian population in Ottoman Empire vary between 1,056,000 and 1,555,000. In the letter that he sent to the French foreign minister, Boghos Nubar Pasha, the Armenian delegate at the Paris Peace Conference, says that after the war, 280,000 Armenians were still living in Turkey and that 600,000 to 700,000 were deported during the war. The delegate claims that 390,000 of those who were deported arrived at their destinations, which means that the number of those who died on the way is about 300,000.

Turkey strongly opposes the use of the term genocide to characterize the deportation of Armenians and the related incidents. Peaceful deportation and the provision of military protection, food, clothing, and shelter on the way had been ordered. At the final destination points, deportees were to be supplied with land and housing commensurate with their previous status. (Ottoman Government Decree, May 1915.) Note that this was not a public decree issued for propaganda purposes, but a secret military document. In his book *Death and Exile/The Ethnic Cleansing of Ottoman Turks* (1995, Princeton, New Jersey), American historian Justin McCarthy argues that the Turkish security forces took the orders for the safe conduct of Armenians seriously, and 2,000 of those who attacked Armenians were killed or imprisoned by the Turkish government.

The official Turkish viewpoint is that Armenians suffered during the years of First World War but that the suffering was mutual and not ordered by the Ottoman government. Some eminent historians, such as Prof. Bernard Lewis of Princeton University and Prof. Gilles Veinstein of College de France, have supported this view. Rather than challenging these historians on academic grounds, Armenians have chosen to take them to court.

After the First World War, allied occupation forces in Istanbul carried out an extensive search for Ottoman government documents that could be used to prove genocide claims. However, no such documents were found. No charges could be brought against Ottoman leaders who were exiled to and imprisoned in Malta with the intention of setting up a trial against them with accusations of genocide. The British Ambassador to Washington, Sir Craigie, reported to foreign minister Lord Curzon, on July 13, 1921, "I am sorry to inform you that there is no evidence that can be used against the Turks in Malta."

Nevertheless, official reports prepared by Allied investigators in the area were based almost exclusively on the allegations of local Armenians and were therefore biased against Turks. Reports about ethnic cleansing of Turks were suppressed. The famous historian Arnold Toynbee wrote a book on the subject, based on biased allegations. The secret propaganda bureau of the British Intelligence funded the book. (Justin McCarthy, *Death and Exile/The Ethnic Cleansing of Ottoman Turks*, 1995, Princeton, New Jersey.)

If there was no genocide, why did so many Armenians die on the way to Lebanon? The reasons are partly cold, disease, and hunger, and partly the attacks carried out by locals. All ethnic hostilities were loose in the area as a result of the ethnic cleansing previously undertaken by Russians and Armenians under Russian occupation. Three million civilian Moslems and Jews had lost their lives during the ethnic cleansing undertaken by the Armenians and the Russians in the east and also by the Greeks in the west. Half the Jews living in western Turkey disappeared under Greek occupation.

Claims for a Homeland: Extremist Armenians claim eastern Turkey as their "homeland." Such claims are not justified by historical facts.

1. At the end of the First World War, Armenians did not constitute the majority in the lands that they claim as their homeland. According to a French document dated 1896, Armenians constituted only 13% of the population in the Ottoman provinces in eastern Turkey. In 1878, after the Ottoman defeat at the Turkish-Russian war, the Armenian Patriarch's request for the British government to support Armenian claims for a homeland in eastern Turkey were denied by the British Ambassador in Istanbul. He told the Patriarch that the Armenians did not have a majority in any single one of the provinces that they claimed were in Armenia.

2. Eastern Anatolia is not the historical homeland of Armenians. There are various theories about the origins of the Armenians. According to the Biblical theory, Armenians are descended from Noah. This is not a scientific theory and therefore not valid. According to another theory, Armenians are descendants of Urartus, a people who lived in eastern Turkey between 3000–600 BC. This theory is not valid either, since there are no similarities between the Armenian and Urartu cultures; In addition, Armenian language belongs to the Satem group of Indo-European languages, whereas the Urartu language belongs to the Ural-Altay group. The name "Armenian" appears for the first time in history at 521 BC in the Behistan inscription of the Persian Emperor Darius: "I defeated the Armenians." Darius met the Armenians in the Caucasus. However, Armenians are not related to the other Caucasian races. The most widely accepted theory about the origin of Armenians is that they descended from a Thracian-Phyrgian group that originated in the Balkans and migrated to Anatolia during the eighth century BC because of the pressure of the Illyrians.

RELATIONS WITH GREECE

Cyprus Issue: There are two communities in Cyprus. 30% of the population is of Turkish origin and 70% of Greek. The island gained its independence from Great Britain in 1960. According to the Zurich and London agreements signed before the island gained its independence, Turkey, Greece, and Britain were given the status of guarantor countries with the right to carry out a unilateral military intervention if the constitutional order was broken. The constitution of the newly independent republic divided the seats in the parliament and in the cabinet and government positions between the two communities.

In 1964, attacks were carried out against the Turks on Cypress by extremist Greeks led by the EOKA, an organization committed to the idea of ENOSIS—union of the island with Greece. EOKA attacks forced Turks throughout the island to live in ghettos and enclaves.

In 1974, a coup was carried out by Nikos Sampson, who had been an EOKA terrorist, and the constitutional president Makarios was ousted. Sampson's coup was a clear breach of constitutional order. Turkey requested the other guarantor countries, Greece and Britain, to jointly intervene in order to restore the constitutional order on the island. Both countries declined Turkey's offer and Turkey carried out an intervention on her own.

Since 1974, Cypress has been divided into two sections: the Turks in the north and the Greeks in the south. Talks are being carried out between the two communities in order to find a final solution to the problem. The Turkish side demands a confederated state based on mutual sovereignty and with restrictions on the rights of the members of either community to travel, to own property, and to run businesses in the federal state of the other community.

The granting of "candidate for full membership" status to southern Cyprus by the EU further complicates the issue. Turkey claims that the EU took this decision under pressure by Greece, which threatened to veto the candidacy of central European nations, which Germany wishes to see as full members. According to London and Zurich agreements, Cyprus cannot join any international organization of which Turkey and Greece are not full members. Turkey has warned that she will further strengthen her relations with the Turkish northern Cyprus if the EU should grant southern Cyprus full membership.

Toward the end of 2001, there was a seeming breakthrough in the relations between the two communities, and direct talks were started between Glafkos Cleridis, president of the Greek Cyprus, and Rauf Denktash, president of the northern enclave in the north. Both leaders attended the talks in their capacity as community leaders.

The Aegean Disputes: There are five sources of conflict between Turkey and Greece in the Aegean:

1. The Continental Shelf: Greece claims the right to explore for oil on the continental shelf of the Aegean islands. Turkey also claims the right to the Aegean continental shelf, since Greek islands sit on Turkey's

continental shelf. In its ruling on September 11, 1976, the International Court of Justice considered the Aegean continental shelf as an "area in dispute." UN Security Council Resolution 395, adopted on August 25, 1976, asked Turkey and Greece to carry out negotiations in order to eliminate their differences with respect to the continental shelf issue. According to an agreement signed between the two countries in Bern on November 11, 1976, the two countries have agreed to suspend their exploration for oil in the Aegean and to negotiate.

2. Territorial Waters: At the moment, the extent of territorial waters is six miles for both countries. This gives 7.5% of the Aegean to Turkey, 43.5% to Greece, and leaves the remaining 49% as high seas. The government of Greece has received authorization from parliament to double the breadth of its country's territorial waters. This would turn the Aegean into a Greek sea and, therefore, not only Turkey but also other Black Sea countries have declared their opposition to such a move.

3. Airspace: According to Articles 1 and 2 of the 1944 Chicago Convention on civil aviation, the extent of national airspace has to correspond to the extent of the country's territorial sea. However, Greece claims a ten-mile airspace regardless of the fact that the extent of her territorial sea is only six miles.

4. Military Activity in Eastern Islands: Greece has been militarizing the eastern islands in the Aegean in open breach of the 1923 Lausanne and 1947 Paris treaties that govern the status of the islands.

5. The Status of Rocks and Islets: In 1996, a new conflict emerged between Turkey and Greece with regard to the status of rocks and islets that are beyond three miles of the Turkey's shore but within Turkey's six miles of territorial waters. According to the Lausanne Peace Treaty, Turkey has given up claim to islands in the Aegean that are beyond three miles of the Turkish shore. However, Turkey claims that this commitment doesn't cover the tiny, uninhabited (and not habitable!) rocks and islets that are beyond 3 miles of the Turkish shore but within Turkey's six mile territorial waters. The issue is important because if such rocks and islets were accepted as Greek territory, the boundary between the two nations would be the middle line passing through them and the Turkish shore, thereby moving the boundary closer to Turkey and reducing the extent of Turkey's territorial waters.

More specifically, the issue came up with regard to the status of the twin rocks of Kardak (Imia in Greek) near Bodrum in southwestern Turkey. A Turkish boat went ashore on one of these rocks in spring 1996, which brought up the issue of their ownership. Greece claimed that Turkey had given up her claims on these rocks according to the

Lausanne Peace Treaty and according to an agreement signed between Turkey and Italy when the Dodecanese Islands belonged to Italy. Turkey claims that the commitment made at Lausanne does not cover rocks and islets, and that the agreement with Italy is not binding according to international law. The agreement with Italy was signed on December 28, 1932, by a low-ranking Turkish Foreign Ministry official and by the Italian military attaché in Ankara. However, the agreement was never registered with the League of Nations as required by international law and never went through the approval procedures required by Turkish internal law and therefore is not valid. That it is not valid has been verified by the appeals to Turkey of Italy in 1935 and of Greece in 1950 and 1953 (after the signing of the 1947 peace treaty which gave the Dodecanese Islands to Greece) inviting Turkey to negotiations to determine the status of the rocks and islets between Turkey and the Dodecanese Islands, and also, by the objection by the USSR to a reference to this agreement at the 1947 Paris Peace Conference, claiming that it is not legally binding according to international law.

Turks in Western Thrace: Following the First World War, Turkey was partitioned amongst the allies, with the western regions of the country given to the Greeks. Turkey's Independence War, which ended in 1923, liberated the country, Moslem Turks living in southern Greece were exchanged with the Christian Greeks living in Turkey. Moslem Turks in northern Greece (western Thrace) and the Greeks living in Istanbul were exempted from the exchange.

Articles 38 to 48 of the Lausanne Treaty give considerable autonomy to the Turks living in northern Greece (Western Thrace). However, the Greek government does not allow the Turkish community to exercise such rights. For example, on paper, the Turkish community has the right to elementary and secondary education in Turkish. However day-care centers in Turkish villages have Greek instructors in order to assimilate children. Core courses in elementary school are taught in Greek. Only 3% of Turkish students in western Thrace can attend Turkish high schools. 12,000 do not have textbooks in Turkish. The books sent by Turkey in 1993 for the consumption of students in Turkish community schools were inspected by the Greek government for eight years. Qualified Turkish teachers are not hired. The compulsory-education requirement, which is nine years in Greece, is not applied to Turks. Moslem religious education among Turks is promoted by the Greek government to limit the number of Turks who will qualify for a college education. Even though there are no legal restrictions, students who are ethnic Turks seldom enter Greek universities since the quality of education they receive has been deliberately kept below the level considered acceptable for university admission.

A special legal mechanism set up during early 1970s by the military government for the persecution of ethnic Turks was maintained for many years by successive civilian Greek governments. According to the arrangements made by the military government, the nineteenth clause of the Greek citizenship would allow the government to deprive her citizens of non-Greek ethnic background of citizenship, if they were suspected of leaving the country not intending to return. This article of the law was annulled under EU pressure in 1998. However, 130,000 ethnic Turks who were stripped of their Greek citizenship under this law are not allowed to return home and they are living in scattered exile in various European countries.

40,000 ethnic Turks living in 118 villages inhabit the area between the Nestos and Evros rivers, encompassing parts of Xanthi, Rodopi, and Evros prefectorates; it is virtually a reservation, "a restricted military zone" with entry and exit subject to the permit of the military. Ethnic Turks living in this area are not only deprived of their basic human rights to travel within their own country but are also relegated to wretched economic and social conditions—even when compared with ethnic Turks living elsewhere in Greece.

There are other forms of oppression of the Turkish minority in western Thrace: There are restrictions on performances by artists from Turkey in the Turkish-populated zones of Greece and on visits to northern Greece by Turkish relatives. Turks are not allowed into public service. Turks are not allowed to serve as officers. No Turk has risen to be a prominent artist or athlete in Greece, although many Greek citizens have done so in Turkey. For many years, Turkish pharmacists were not allowed to start businesses of their own, and Turks were not allowed to work as taxi drivers for "national security" reasons. Turks were denied drivers' licenses and permits to buy guns. Economic standards of Turks are far below those of Greeks. Most members of the Turkish community in Greece are farmers. However, it used to be very difficult for a Turk to buy a tractor. Also, Turks are required to have permits in order to buy land. The Greek government carries out a policy of expropriating the land owned by the community. In 1923, the Turkish community in Greece owned 85% of the land in western Thrace. Today, they own only 35%.

Regardless of the fact that the Treaty of Lausanne (1923) grants the Turkish minority the right to organize and conduct its own religious affairs, since 1985 the government has directly appointed—against the wishes of the overwhelming majority of ethnic Turks—the community's muslim religious leaders, the *muftis*. This situation was codified in the December 1990 Law No. 1920. Currently, there are two *muftis* in the cities of Xanthi and Komotini; one appointed and one elected. The elected *mufti* of Xanthi, Mehmet Emin Aga, has accumulated 82 months of prison in nine trials since June 1996 for merely using the title of *mufti* in written statements.

Greek Law No. 1091 (1980) and Presidential Decree No. 1 (1991) are designed to limit the Turkish community's control over and to financially weaken the Turkish private charitable foundations (known in Turkish as *vakif*), which support minority education, social welfare, and other activities.

There are similar problems related to the repairing and building of mosques. As regards the construction or repair of mosques, the situation has improved since 1992. However, the Turkish minority still must overcome considerable bureaucratic obstacles before obtaining construction permits. In September 1996, as soon as a building permit for "an annex to a mosque" at Kimmeria was granted, there were protests from ultra nationalists, which resulted in the December 1996 arrest of 23 individuals for "arbitrary construction with violations." The sentences given ranged from 35 days to four months and were all suspended on appeal. In mid 1997, the *imam* was allowed to finish the repair of the mosque, though not to build the new minaret to the desired height.

The most important form of oppression against Turks in Greece is that they are not recognized as Turks and therefore deprived of minority rights (Yalcin Bayer, *Hürriyet,* June 20, 2001). The Greek government claims that in Articles 38 to 48 of the Lausanne Treaty, Turks of western Thrace are referred to as "Moslems" and not as "Turks." However, in Protocol Number 6, the section of the Treaty that determines the conditions of exchange of the Greek population in Turkey with the Turkish population in Greece, Muslim residents of western Thrace are clearly referred to as "Turks" who will not be included in the exchange of populations along with the "Greeks" in Istanbul. Also, administrative orders issued by the Greek government in the 1950s recognize the Moslem minority in western Thrace as Turks.

In July 1998, primary school teacher Rasim Hint was suspended from teaching for one year because, in 1996, he had called the Xanthi School where he worked a "Turkish" rather than a "minority" school. For the same reason, Hint was subjected to punitive transfers from the city of Xanthi to distant mountain villages between 1996–1998. Twelve Turkish teachers who mentioned the name Turk in a public declaration were sentenced to seven-year jail terms in 1997. Usually, these sentences are converted to monetary payments with the threat that they will be executed if the crime is repeated. Such action is aimed at pacifiying the activists.

In January 1990, Dr. Sadik Ahmet, a former member of the Greek parliament from Komotini, was sentenced to 18 months imprisonment by a Greek court because he had referred to himself as a "Turk" in his election pamphlet. Following the imprisonment of Dr. Sadik Ahmet, houses and shops belonging to Turks in Komotini were raided and several Turks were beaten by mobs of extremist Greeks. A similar incident had taken place against the Greeks in Istanbul in 1955. However, in Turkey, those responsible for this episode were eventually brought to trial and sentenced; none were in Greece. Dr. Sadik Ahmet eventually lost his life in a traffic accident, which Turks claim was an assassination.

The number of Turks living western Thrace is 150,000. Turks make up 35% of the population in the area where they live. There were 125,000 Turks in western Thrace, making up 67% of the population, when the Lausanne Treaty was signed. It is estimated that this number would now have been 600,000 had Turks not been led to emigrate under various pressures.

Recent Developments: Relations between Turkey and Greece had deteriorated under Greek Prime Minister Andreas Papandreou but improved under his successor Smitis, with the son of former Papandreou, Yorgo Papandreou, as the Greek Foreign Minister. The earthquake Turkey experienced provided the background for the improvement of relations between the two nations. Greeks came to Turkey's aid on a large scale, and Turkey reciprocated with aid to the earthquake experienced in Athens a few months later. Greece lifted her veto on the delivery of most of EU funds for Turkey and her objection to Turkey becoming a candidate member. Warm relations were established between the Greek Foreign Minister Yorgo Papandreou and Turkey's Foreign Minister Ismail Cem. Military flights over the Aegean are suspended. However, as of Spring 2002, no progress was made on any of the key issues that are the sources of conflict. Schengen Visas issued to Turks, which were valid in all EU countries, were not valid in Greece. According to the Turkish Foreign Ministry, only 94 out of the 2,500 news and articles that appeared in the Greek press on the topic of Turkish-Greek relations during the first six months of 2000 were favorable toward Turkey. During the same period, 85% of the news and articles that appeared in the Turkish press were favorable toward Greece.

EUROPEAN UNION MEMBERSHIP

History of Turkey's Relations with the EU: Turkey is the only Muslim candidate nation of the EU. Most Turks regard eventual EU membership as the final chapter of the modernization process that was set in motion by the founding father of the Republic, Mustafa Kemal

Ataturk. An agreement was signed between Turkey and the EU as early as 1963 in anticipation of full membership, and Turkey has lifted customs with Europe since 1995. However, at the EU summit held in Luxembourg in December 1997, Turkey was not included in the list of prospective members of the Union. In the Luxembourg communiqué, Poland, Hungary, Czech Republic, Slovenia, Estonia, and Southern Cyprus were granted the status of "candidate for full membership," with Lithuania, Bulgaria, Romania, Slovakia, and Latvia to follow. Turkey was termed "as eligible as others." As *The Economist* (December 20, 1997) pointed out, in this case, "equal eligibility evidently did not mean equal treatment."

Many of the countries that were granted the status of "candidate nation" in Luxembourg were not even in existence when relations were established between Turkey and EU in 1963, and many others were Warsaw Pact members. Turkey, on the other hand, has been of key importance for the Western alliance and a member of NATO since 1951. Critics of the EU approach voiced the question whether it would have been easier for Turkey to join the EU if Turkey been a former Warsaw Pact member. Critics also pointed out that it was a strategic mistake for the EU to leave out a very rapidly growing economy such as Turkey and a metropolis such as Istanbul, which is a major centre of attraction for North Africa, the Middle East, Balkans, and the Black Sea. Besides, Turkey is a corridor to Central Asia and the Caucuses. In 1997, in terms of the economic criteria accepted by the EU, Turkey was ahead of all central and east European countries, which were recognized as candidates. (Center de Relations Europeans, *La Turquie, 10 Ans Aprens sa Demande d'Adhesion a l'Union Europeene*, p. 120 –121.)

Following the Luxembourg summit, Turkey suspended all political contacts with the EU, became critical of the customs union arrangements with the EU, and intensified her relations with the US and Israel. Relations were further impaired when EU leaders declared that they would grant Greek Cyprus membership before Turkey becomes a member. Turkey claims that according to the 1959 and 1960 London and Zurich agreements, Cyprus cannot join any international organization of which Turkey is not also a member.

The EU remedied the situation by declaring Turkey a "candidate" at the summit held in Helsinki in 1999, two years after the Luxembourg summit. However, at the following summit held in Cannes, Turkey was not included in the EU plans for expansion for the present decade.

As of 2002, Turkey was in the "pre-negotiation" stage of the accession process. Membership talks between Turkey and EU were in progress, but at a much slower rate when compared with other candidate nations. The EU had aims to complete negotiations with ten candidates, namely the Greek Cypriot Administration, Malta, Czech Republic, Estonia, Hungary, Latvia, Lithuania, Poland, Slovakia, and Slovenia in 2002. Those countries will become full members of the union by 2005 at the latest. Bulgaria and Romania are expected to join a few years later. As of 2002, in order not to miss the EU train forever, Turkey was hoping to start the "screening" process, which takes place before the EU starts accession negotiations with a candidate country, in the year 2004, five years after receiving the status of candidate. That the screening process had not started by 2002 could be a sign of discriminative policy towards Turkey.

For the screening process to start, the EU provides the candidate country with a detailed version of its *acquis communautaire,* which is an agenda that details the various legislative and other measures which need to be implemented to bring candidate country's laws and regulations in line with those prevailing in the EU. To judge from the progress made by the current 12 countries in negotiation, reaching agreement on the *acquis* will take, at best, a minimum of three years. Allowing two years for post-negotiation ratification, Turkish accession looks unlikely before 2010, some two or three years after the "best guess" accession date for Bulgaria and Romania, which are likely to be the last of the current twelve aspirants to be admitted.

Issues: Opponents of Turkey's EU membership fear that Turkey would impose a big financial burden reaching up to 20–30 billion Euros a year on the EU budget. However, if Turkey joins the EU, the total support Turkey would receive from the EU budget will be no more than 10 billion Euros (6 billion Euros in structural support and 4 billion Euros in agricultural support). This amount equals merely 0.15% of the total GNP of EU countries (Onur Oymen, *Turkiye'nin Gucu).* Since Turkey would contribute roughly 3 billion Euros to the EU budget, net EU support for Turkey would be no more than 7 billion Euros (Faruk Sen and Cigdem Akkaya, *Cumhuriyet,* 9/2/2000).

Turkey's large population (65 million) is often pointed out as an obstacle on the way to full membership in the EU. Yet, the total population of Romania and Poland, which are candidates for full membership, is also 60 million. Turkey's large population may prove to be an asset in the long run. Between 1999–2025, 7 of the 15 European Union countries will experience a drop in population. The highest drop will be in Italy with 6 million. The population of Spain will drop by 2.9 million, of Germany by 2, Greece by 0.7, Portugal by 0.6, Belgium by 0.3, and Denmark by 0.1. During the same period, the population of France will rise by 2.8 million, of the UK by 1.3, and of Ireland by 0.7. The overall change in the European population will be a drop of 7.3

million. (Source: Eurostat.) Turkey's population will rise by 22.4 million during the same period. This young Turkish population may be welcome in the EU as labor force and also as consumers.

Nevertheless, Europe probably considers the influx of Turkish workers as a potential problem. Former German Chancellor Kohl once stated to Turkey's president at the time, Suleyman Demirel, that it would be impossible for him to deal with 10 million Turks in Germany—which is the number he thought would move to Germany if Turkey became a full member. German Foreign Minister Kinkel was quoted to have said at the Luxembourg summit that Germany, which already has 2.1 million Turks, couldn't allow a further influx. (Jean Quatremer, *Liberation*, October 27, 1997.)

Prospective members of the EU are required to satisfy various economic and political criteria in order to qualify for full membership. The Maastricht Treaty defines economic criteria; the political criteria are summarized under the title "Copenhagen Criteria."

According to the Maastricht Treaty signed by EU member countries, public deficit should be less than 3% and public debt should be less than 60% of GNP. Currently, these figures are 12% and 90% for Turkey. Again, the Maastricht Treaty brings upper limits for inflation and interest rates for member countries. The upper limit for inflation rate is defined to be no more than 1.5% over the average inflation rate of the three lowest-inflation countries. The upper limit for interest rates is defined to be no more 2% over the average interest rate for the three lowest-interest-rate countries. Presently, Turkey is far from meeting these criteria. However, many of the candidate nations and some members do not meet some of the criteria either. For example, public debt of Greece is equal to 100% of her GNP. However, the Greek economy enjoys massive EU support. Turkey's economic problems are possibly exacerbated by lack of similar support by the EU.

On the political front, EU candidate countries are required to satisfy the so-called "Copenhagen criteria," which stipulate "stability of institutions guaranteeing democracy, the rule of law, human rights, and the respect for and protection of minorities."

Turkey has made progress towards satisfying these criteria. On October 3, 2001, the parliament adopted a package of 34 amendments to the constitution, several of which were specifically formulated with the Copenhagen criteria in mind. There were also numerous legislative changes, some of which were in the area of judicial reform. The composition of the National Security Council was changed so that the council now has a civilian majority and is more advisory in nature. A number of restrictions on civil liberties (freedom of expression, press, and association) were removed. Limitations were introduced on the use of the death penalty. These long overdue reforms were welcomed and seen as a major step forward. In 2002, the primary agenda of the parliament is to enact further legislative changes necessary to implement the constitutional reforms. Steps on the independence of the judiciary and the adoption of the new Turkish criminal law are also expected. The revision of the controversial state tender law, which is designed to prevent widespread corruption, is also on the agenda of the Parliament.

The EU also has demands in the area of human rights. Turkey has ratified fewer than half of the human rights conventions the EU requires its candidates to adopt. The other candidate countries have ratified the bulk of these. The EU also demands the introduction of Kurdish language education and Kurdish TV. Many Turks fail to believe the sincerity of such demands, particularly when one considers the condition of certain minorities in Europe, such as the Turkish minority in Greece.

International Issues: Solution of the Cyprus problem and the easing of the tension with Greece are also presented as prerequisites for membership of Turkey in the EU, even though no such requirements were set for Greece and for Greek Cypriots.

According to a decision taken at the EU summit held in Helsinki in 1999, the year 2004 is the deadline for Turkey and Greece to end their disputes with regard to the Aegean. The two nations are to negotiate up to that date and take the matter to the International Court in The Hague if they have not received a consensus by then. This decision may be difficult to implement since Greece refuses to recognize the existence of any issues in the Aegean except for the continental shelf issue, rendering negotiations envisaged in Helsinki virtually impossible. Nevertheless, talks were resumed between the two nations in 2002.

With regard to the admission of Cyprus to the EU, the EU has so far negotiated solely with the Greek Cypriot authorities. However, the EU would probably prefer to admit Cyprus after the resolution of the long-standing conflict that divides the island. But Greece, which assumes the EU's rotating presidency for the first half of 2003, threatens to block the whole enlargement process unless Greek Cyprus is admitted. This means that the EU is likely to admit Greek Cyprus before an agreement is reached between the Greek and Turkish Cypriots. In response, the Turkish government has threatened to annex the northern part of Cyprus, which would set Ankara on a collision course with the EU and could irreversibly set back Turkey's own membership prospects. In the meantime, both Turks and Greeks are under pressure by both the EU and the US to settle the dispute. Serious negotiations were resumed between the Greek and Turkish Cypriot community leaders in January 2002.

Turkey's stance on the proposed European Security and Defense Force (ESDF) has also been a source of friction between Turkey and the EU. The nub of the issue is that the EU wants guaranteed access to NATO assets and planning facilities for the ESDF and wants Turkish troops to serve with the ESDF, but it also wishes to keep Turkey, a NATO member, out of decision making. Turkey demands a say in decision-making for the force in which it will participate, and it demands to retain the right to veto the use of NATO assets. The final agreement reached between the US, the UK, and Turkey, pending approval by Greece, involves assurances that the ESDF will not be deployed in Cyprus or the Aegean; in addition, Turkey will be consulted with regard to action that will take place in regions that Turkey considers to be directly related to her own security interests.

Prospects: Annual financial contributions Turkey would qualify for, as a full member of the EU, would equal half the loan the country received from the IMF in 2002. Also, under the present arrangements, if she were to become a member of EU, because of her large population, Turkey would have 74 out of 788 seats in the European Parliament, which would make hers the largest representation. As a full member of the EU, Turkey would be awarded 29 seats as well in the European Commission.

Turkish supporters of EU membership point out these concrete advantages and favor the fulfillment of EU demands from Turkey in the area of domestic and international politics. Critics point out, however, that EU will never admit Turkey to full membership precisely because the potential gains Turkey will experience vis-à-vie existing members are so great. The statement in the *EU Strategy Paper* released on November 13, 2001, that "in practice, the immediate question for Turkey is not whether it will be able to achieve full membership of the EU, but whether it is ready to adopt EU standards on both political and economic fronts on their own merits," is interpreted by critics as a sign of the unwillingness of the EU to admit Turkey to full membership.

A recent study shows that 60% of Turks believe that the EU will never admit Turkey to full membership no matter what. 80% of Turks are opposed to making concessions on issues that they believe concern "national sovereignty." 78.5% regard EU demands on Kurdish TV and education, Cyprus, and Armenian genocide allegations as infringements on national sovereignty aimed at splitting Turkey. (Metin Aydogan, Mudafa-i Hukuk Dergisi, quoted by Umit Zileli, *Cumhuriyet*, August 30, 2001, p. 17.)

Critics believe that the real reasons behind the EU's reluctance to admit Turkey are perhaps cultural and religious. European Christian Democrats declared at their summit in Spring 1997 that Turkey could not be European for "cultural and religious" reasons (Michael Luders, *Die Zeit,* October 24, 1997). The Foreign Affairs Committee Chairman of the EU once stated that the Union has never been candid with Turkey. "We have been fooling them. The EU has no intention of having Turks as members." (Emin Colasan, *Hurriyet,* 13/7/2000). Jurgen Ruttgers, the deputy chairman of the German Christian Democrats, reiterated similar views in December 2002. *(Welt am Sonntag,* December 9, 2001).

Presently, there is disagreement amongst EU nations with regard to expansion in general. The extreme right government in Austria opposes further expansion of the EU. Poorer EU members like Spain, Portugal, and Greece fear that the expansion of the EU will reduce the aid they receive from the union. 80% of the EU budget is spent on agricultural support policy and on aid to poorer nations. Countries like Germany fear the "social costs of expansion." Basically, Germany already faces ethnic problems, and is afraid that it will be flooded with new migrants. Germany would therefore prefer to deny the right for the "free movement of labor" for prospective members. Also, Germany desires Europe to become a true federal state, whereas France would prefer a confederation.

Expansion issues are being debated at the newly formed European Convention, of which Turkey is also member, together with other candidate nations. The Convention is headed by former French President Giscard d'Estaing, an outspoken opponent of Turkey's membership.

INDEX

www.ingramcontent.com/pod-product-compliance
Lightning Source LLC
Chambersburg PA
CBHW030024290326
41934CB00005B/476